U0565237

中华优秀传统文化书系

孟子

（三）

Excellent Chinese Traditional Culture
The Works of Mencius

本书编写组 编

山東畫報出版社

山东是儒家文化的发源地，也是中华优秀传统文化的重要发祥地，在灿烂辉煌的中华传统文化“谱系”中占有重要地位。用好齐鲁文化资源丰富的优势，扎实推进中华优秀传统文化研究阐发、保护传承和传播交流，推动中华优秀传统文化创造性转化、创新性发展，是习近平总书记对山东提出的重大历史课题、时代考卷，也是山东坚定文化自信、守护中华民族文化根脉的使命担当。

为挖掘阐发、传播普及以儒家思想为代表的中华优秀传统文化，推动中华文明与世界不同文明交流互鉴，山东省委宣传部组织策划了“中华优秀传统文化书系”，并列入山东省优秀传统文化传承发展工程重点项目。书系以儒家经典“四书”（《大学》《中庸》《论语》《孟子》）为主要内容，对儒家文化蕴含的哲学思想、人文精神、教化思想、道德理念等进行了现代性阐释。书系采用权威底本、精心校点、审慎译注，同时添加了权威英文翻译和精美插图，是兼具历史性与时代性、民族性与国际性、学术性与普及性、艺术性与实用性于一体的精品佳作。

《孟子》是记录孟子及其弟子言行以及孟子游说各国国君、同各派思想家进行辩论的语录体著作。它集中反映了孟子的思想体系，同时保留了不少战国时期的历史信息，为我们理解孟子、走进百家争鸣那个时代提供了基本材料。

一、孟子其人其书

孟子，名轲，战国时期邹（今山东邹城）人。相传孟子是鲁国贵族孟孙氏后裔，幼年丧父，家庭贫穷，迁居至邹，由其母抚养长大。

孟子是继孔子、曾子、子思之后儒家学派又一位重要人物，被后世誉为“亚圣”，与孔子并称“孔孟”。其生卒年不见详载，杨伯峻考证为约公元前385年到公元前304年。孟子在书中说：“予未得为孔子徒也，予私淑诸人也。”孟子以继承孔子衣钵为己任，但未能言明其师是何人。关于孟子之师，学界有所争论，但多以《史记·孟子荀卿列传》所载为是，即“受业子思之门人”，也就是说孟子是孔子的孙子——子思的再传弟子，可谓是儒门正宗。所以其书以继承发扬孔子的思想为要，正所谓“退而与万章之徒序《诗》《书》，述仲尼之意，作《孟子》七篇”。

《孟子》的主要内容来源于孟子自是无疑，可其具体作者，学界有不同认识，比如孟子自著；孟子门下弟子万章和公孙丑之徒在孟子死后所著等，其中以在孟子生前由弟子辅助所著最能为人接受。《史记》记载《孟子》为七篇，而应劭《风俗通义·穷通篇》却说：“退与万章之徒序《诗》《书》，仲尼之意，作书中、外十一篇。”《汉书·艺文志》也著录“《孟子》十一篇”。赵岐以《外书》四篇为伪，故不为之作注，后世研读者日少，逐渐亡佚。到了明代，姚士粦又伪撰《孟子外书》四篇，清人周广业指斥其“显属伪托”，梁启超则以其为“伪中出伪”。

《孟子》七篇，每篇分上下，计十四卷二百六十章，总计三万五千余字，是“四书”中部头最大、内容最丰富的一本。但长期以来《孟子》一直处于子书或传文位置，直到五代十国时期后蜀诏刻十一经将其列入，后宋太宗加以翻刻，《孟子》才开始进入经书行列。到南宋朱熹把《论语》《大学》《中庸》《孟子》合刊编写《四书章句集注》，《孟子》更加受到学者重视，孟子的思想也更大程度上影响了中国古代思想史的进程。

二、《孟子》之思想

《孟子》一书思想宏大、细致入微，主要反映了孟子本人及其同时代人的人性论、政治思想，以及孟子本人独特的经济思想、生态观、工夫论，其中涵盖了其与时人的义利（欲）之辩、人禽之辩、性命之辩、心体之辩等诸多内容。但由于其语录体的展开形式，孟子的同一思想多散落到各篇的许多章中，我们在理解的时候要仔细爬梳，把同一主题的全部相关内容放到一起进行综合判断，而不能一叶障目、断章取义。

人性论　人性论是先秦诸子乃至整个中国思想史的核心论题，孟子的人性论更是其思想体系的出发点和终极依据。孟子的人性论是通过其与告子的辩论展开的，主要见于《告子上》一篇。告子认为“性无善无不善”，其时还有人认为“性可以为善，可以为不善”，后来荀子则力主性恶论，与此相对，孟子的人性论为性善论。这些都是继孔子“性相近”之后的不同阐发路径。

孟子“性善论”之“性”是指人之异于禽兽的“几希”之性，而不是作为实然起点的与生俱来的性的全部；其“善”则是指道德意义上的正向发挥。孟子证明性善是通过心善来完成的，以心善言性善，即本心在摆脱生理欲望后自主呈现的善，是人之所以为人的道德主体，是性善的根本依据。所以其有涵盖恻隐之心、羞恶之心、恭敬之心、是非之心的“四心”说，并以此四心为仁、义、礼、智四德之端，由此说明“四心”“四德”皆“非由外铄我也，我固有之也”。需要注意的是孟子并不认为四德是齐一的，而仍是以“仁”为统领的。既然性是善的，那恶又从何而来？孟子认为人受于耳目物欲之蔽而丧失其本心，恶由是而生。告子认为“食色性也”，但孟子认为耳目之欲一类虽从与生俱来意义上是为性的，而从其实现意义上则取决于外，是有命的，故人的本心是会被物欲所蔽而最终失于流放的，所以“君子不谓性也”。既然恶能产生，我们又当如何处理呢？

孟子提出“求其放心”的方法论。“放心”就是被物欲“引之”而流失的本心，若要回归本性之善，必须找回此“放心”，使其复如原态。此一过程全由人的自觉意识和自主行动主宰，所以孟子的性善论既是对人的价值的肯定，也推动了人主体自由的崛起和心灵自主的实现，正如其所说“万物皆备于我”，以及“舍我其谁”的自信精神。

性情关系是孟子人性论的又一重要论述，“乃若其情，则可以为善矣，乃所谓善也”，其意为情理并非经验，应然未必实然，价值根源于主体自觉，实现价值的能力就在性善的本质之中。孟子的人性论是和天命论相伴而行的，其内在逻辑为“尽其心者，知其性也；知其性，则知天矣”。由此而衍生出“存其心，养其性，所以事天也”的工夫论。

工夫论　孟子的工夫论可以概括为：存心、养性、集义、养浩然之气。存心、养性皆直接出自其性善论，前文已交代明白，此处，外加一条便是防范本心之失的根本措施——寡欲。

孟子极为注重集义，不仅与告子进行义内义外的辩论，而且直言“礼门义路”，把践行仁义作为人生唯一的根本正途。由集义而生养浩然之气，浩然之气至大至刚，就是“集义所生者”。人性是善的，但社会环境是复杂的，环境的复杂极易导致人性背离本善，所以人人皆需时刻自持。总之，孟子的工夫论就是保养其性善论的方法论，就是扩充四端的根本要求。

政治思想　孟子的政治思想是其思想体系的致用主体部分，也是先秦各家政治思想中的巅峰之作。如萧公权《中国政治思想史》所说：“孟子之政治思想遂成为针对虐政之永久抗议。”孟子直接继承孔子“苛政猛于虎”

的批判，针对“民之憔悴于虐政”的现实情况，孟子把孔子仁的思想具体发展成为切于时弊的仁政思想。孟子仁政思想的巨大贡献在于其扭转了政治思想中的君民关系，把统治者为政治意志统领的位置转变为一切以人民的意志为根据，统治者遂沦为政治的执行者，而人民成为真正的政治归属，即民本思想。

孟子的“民为贵，社稷次之，君为轻”一语道破玄机，成为中国历代君王头上那把高悬的民意之剑。遵循民意也就成了统治者行事的根本出发点，必得以民“所欲与之聚之，所恶勿施尔也”，也就是《梁惠王下》中所说的“国人杀之”。如果统治者不以民意行事，甚至为国作乱、恣意施政，那该怎么处理呢？孟子对此提出了政权转移的学说。齐宣王以为“汤放桀，武王伐纣”是弑君行为，而孟子却说：“贼仁者谓之贼，贼义者谓之残，残贼之人谓之一夫。闻诛一夫纣矣，未闻弑君也。”可见君之为君必得践行仁义，而不能戕害仁义、祸乱百姓，否则君便不再称其君，人人可取而代之。但此一政权转移说被历代统治者解释、执行为双重标准：一方面，在取代上一政权时，批判其违背民意而被自己取代；另一方面，到王朝后期，政治日渐腐败时，自己则对此说讳莫如深。基于此说，孟子在游说各国君主时，常常劝其施行仁政、招揽人心，此所谓“王道”（“王天下”之道）。

由仁政，孟子还提出了与之相关的具体措施，其中蕴含了与民养教、发展经济、保护生态等特色内容。“先王有不忍人之心，斯有不忍人之政矣”，王者要有“天下有溺者，由己溺之也……天下有饥者，由己饥之也”的同情之心，以及在此同情之心的基础上发展出“解民于倒悬”的“不忍人之政”。民众的幸福首先来自生活的富足，所以孟子提出“制民之产”，提出“五亩之宅，树之以桑”“鸡豚狗彘之畜，无失其时”“百亩之田，勿夺其时”“谨庠序之教，申之以孝悌之义”的养教措施。只要统治者肯认真施行，则“黎民不饥不寒”“民养生丧死无憾也”，进而民有所恒产，“有恒产者有恒心”，也就避免了“无恒产者无恒心。苟无恒心，放辟邪侈，无不为已”的混乱局面，如此也就不会“不王”了。

孟子的经济思想进而衍生出了生态保护的思想，即“数罟不入洿池”“斧斤以时入山林”，虽然很难说孟子自主意识里保护自然的思想是成熟的，但这种朴素的主张确实有其重要历史意义。而且孟子经济思想中还兼顾农、工、商诸业。对于农业，他构建了理想化的“井田制”（无论井田制在孟子之前是否施行过，孟子提出的井田制都是一种土地改革意愿式的理想化主张）；对于工商业，他提出“关，市讥而不征”“市，廛而不征，法而不廛”，使其自由发展而不设限。孟子的政治思想博大精深，在战国时期诸侯争霸的时代背景中可谓是一股清流，但其“贵王贱霸”的主张和诸侯国君的利益诉求背道而驰，常被认为是“迂远而阔于事情”，终未被接受和施行，而其在思想史上却具有深远意义，对后世为政者的警醒和对民众的养教也有着不可磨灭的历史贡献。

我们分析孟子思想体系时，尤需注意孟子的人文关怀、现实关怀，注意其以继承发扬孔子思想为己任的使命感，注意其发先圣所未发的创新点，注意其针对“邪说”加以批驳的责任感。其论说多有所指，而非是“好辩”而已。其说：“杨墨之道不息，孔子之道不著，是邪说诬民，充塞仁义也。”

三、七篇贻矩，惠及今日

清雍正皇帝手书“七篇贻矩”金匾，悬挂于山东邹城孟府大堂檐下正中，向人们昭示着孟子著书的伟大功绩和对后世的惠及之恩。本书能将两千多年前孟子的著述再次呈现给读者，并把其中的思想价值进行现代化

阐释，也是我们承担历史接续的光荣。

《孟子》的历史价值　孔子罕言性与命，到子思则大论性命，到了孟子更是把儒家性命论推向了高峰，所以学界有“思孟学派”一说。这一性命论不仅参与了先秦诸子的历史讨论，还直接影响了宋明以来程朱理学、陆王心学的此起彼伏。孟子的政治思想虽未能在当时施行，但其理论进步意义远高于当时指导兼并战争的“合纵连横”思想，而且孟子反对战争，认为“春秋无义战”。孟子的仁政思想其实不是简单的民本主义，其内在确实含有近代民主主义的色彩。自秦以降，中国历代都没能很好地执行孟子政治思想中最为根本的积极因素，甚至某些时候与之背道而驰，与孟子思想比照起来可以说是一种历史的倒退。孟子在其思想中呈现出的伟岸人格为历代读书人所景仰，孟子思想中的永恒意义一直照耀着我们前行的道路。

《孟子》的现实价值　孟子距今已两千

余载，但其思想时刻浮现在我们脑海，其教诲始终萦绕于我们耳边。继承孟子思想是我们的历史责任，发扬孟子哲学是我们的时代使命，所以我们必须深入理解孟子思想，解剖其实质内涵，辨析其根本，进而完成其创造性转化，通过实践使之得到创新性发展。回望身后，其实也照耀着前方的路。孟子思想体系中的积极因素，既有着进行历史研究、哲学研究、政治研究、社会研究的重大学术价值，也有着指导当下实践、启发政治生活、警醒不良之风的实际意义。而这些意义的实现前提是我们要立足当下，科学把握孟子思想，真正把《孟子》读好、读透。

目录 Contents

万章上

Wan Zhang 1

9.1

万章[1]问曰："舜往于田，号泣于旻天[2]，何为其号泣也？"

孟子曰："怨慕[3]也。"

万章曰："'父母爱之，喜而不忘；父母恶之，劳而不怨。'然则舜怨乎？"

曰："长息[4]问于公明高[5]曰：'舜往于田，则吾既得闻命矣；号泣于旻天，于父母，则吾不知也。'公明高曰：'是非尔所知也。'夫公明高以孝子之心，为不若是恝[6]，我竭力耕田，共为子职而已矣，父母之不我爱，于我何哉？帝使其子九男二女，百官牛羊仓廪备，以事舜于畎亩之中。天下之士多就之者，帝将胥[7]天下而迁之焉。为不顺[8]于父母，如穷人无所归。天下之士悦之，人之所欲也，而不足以解忧；好色，人之所欲，妻帝之二女，而不足以解忧；富，人之所欲，富有天下，而不足以解忧；贵，人之所欲，贵为天子，而不足以解忧。人悦之、好色、富贵，无足以解忧者，惟顺于父母，可以解忧。人少，则慕父母；知好色，则慕少艾[9]；有妻子，则慕妻子；仕则慕君，不得于君则热中[10]。大孝终身慕父母。五十而慕者，予于大舜见之矣。”

Wan Zhang asked Mencius, saying, “When Shun went into the fields, he cried out and wept towards the pitying heavens. Why did he cry out and weep?”

Mencius replied, “He was dissatisfied, and full of earnest desire.”

Wan Zhang said, “When his parents love him, a son rejoices and forgets them not. When his parents hate him, though they punish him, he does not murmur. Was Shun then murmuring against his parents?”

Mencius answered, “Chang Xi asked Gongming Gao, saying, 'As to Shun's going into the fields, I have received your instructions, but I do not know about his weeping and crying out to the pitying heavens and to his parents.' Gongming Gao answered him, 'You do not understand that matter.' Now, Gongming Gao supposed that the heart of the filial son could not be so free of sorrow. Shun would say, 'I exert my strength to cultivate the fields, but I am thereby only discharging my office as a son. What can there be in me that my parents do not love me?' The emperor caused his own children, nine sons and two daughters, the various officers, oxen and sheep, storehouses and granaries, all to be prepared, to serve Shun amid the channelled fields. Of the scholars of the kingdom there were multitudes who flocked to him. The sovereign designed that Shun should superintend the kingdom along with him, and then to transfer it to him entirely. But because his parents were not in accord with him, he felt like a poor man who has nowhere to turn to. To be delighted in by all the scholars of the kingdom, is what men desire, but it was not sufficient to remove the sorrow of Shun. The possession of beauty is what men desire, and Shun had for his wives the two daughters of the emperor, but this was not sufficient to remove his sorrow. Riches are what men desire, and the kingdom was the rich property of Shun, but this was not sufficient to remove his sorrow. Honours are what men desire, and Shun had the dignity of being sovereign, but this was not sufficient to remove his sorrow. The reason why the being the object of men's delight, with the possession of beauty, riches, and honours were not sufficient to remove his sorrow, was that it could be removed only by his getting his parents to be in accord with him. The desire of the child is towards his father and mother. When he becomes conscious of the attractions of beauty, his desire is towards young and beautiful women. When he comes to have a wife and children, his desire is towards them. When he obtains office, his desire is towards his sovereign: — if he cannot get the regard of his sovereign, he burns within. But the man of great filial piety, to the end of his life, has his desire towards his parents. In the great Shun I see the case of one whose desire at fifty years was towards them."

【注释】[1]万章：孟子弟子。[2]旻(mín)天：上天。[3]怨慕：自责与思慕。这里是说舜自怨不能让父母对自己满意而思慕得父母之欢心。[4]长息：公明高的弟子。[5]公明高：曾子的弟子。[6]恝(jiá)：无动于衷。[7]胥：皆，尽。[8]顺：爱也。[9]少艾：年轻美貌之人。[10]热中：心热而焦急。

【译文】万章问："舜到田地里劳作，向着仁慈的上天诉说、哭泣，他为什么诉说、哭泣呢？”

孟子说：“因为对父母既抱怨又眷恋。”

万章说：“（曾子说过）‘父母爱自己，高兴但不因此而松懈；父母讨厌自己，劳苦却不因此而怨恨。’那么，舜是怨恨自己的父母吗？”

（孟子）说：“从前长息曾经问过公明高说：‘舜到田里去，我已经懂得了；他向天诉说、哭泣，这样来对待父母，我却还不懂得这是为什么。’公明高说：‘这个事不是你所能懂的。’那公明高认为孝子之心，是不像这般无动于衷，我用尽力气耕田种地，是作为儿子的职责所在罢了，父母不爱儿子，作为儿子能怎么办呢？帝尧让他的九个儿子、两个女儿带着百官、牛羊、粮食到田地里侍奉舜；天下的士人，很多投奔舜的，帝尧准备将天下禅位给舜。舜因为不能让父母顺心，便如同穷困之人一般，无所归往。天下的善士都喜欢他，是人所想要得到的，却不能排解忧愁；美丽的女子，是人所想要得到的，以帝舜的两个女儿为妻，却不能排解忧愁；财富，是人所想要得到的，拥有天下的财富，却不足以排解忧愁；尊贵，是人所想要得到的，尊贵到成为君主，却不足以排解忧愁。士人归心、美丽的女子、财富、尊贵，这些都不足以排解忧愁；只有顺了父母的意愿才可以排解忧愁。人年少的时候，思慕父母；到了懂得（喜欢）美丽的女子的时候，就又思慕年轻而漂亮的人；有了妻子儿女，就又思慕老婆孩子；成为国家官员，就又思慕君主，不获君主宠爱，就又内心焦急而惶恐不已。大孝终身思慕父母，五十岁了依旧思慕父母的人，我从大舜那里见识到了啊。”

【解读】本章通过孟子与弟子万章的谈话，对舜完善人格之中的孝道进行了心理层面的剖析。先圣大舜无疑是中国历史上的一位孝子，面对家人的种种责难甚至戕害，他做到了“顺适不失子道，兄弟孝慈。欲杀，不可得；即求，尝在侧”。史传，大舜得到帝尧的重用后，可谓是名播天下、功成名就，但圣人内心思慕父母的忧愁却久久不能释怀。劳作之余暗自感伤，常常独自“号泣于旻天”，哭诉心中的苦楚。他的这种行为让常人不得其解，孟子认为像舜那样“天下之士悦之”“妻帝之二女”“富有天下”“贵为天子”都不足以解忧，唯有顺了父母的意愿，方可去掉心中挥之不去的痛楚，得到一种解脱。这是一种圣人的孝道，其孝之深、之真，一切爱戴、美色及富贵都是无法取代的。这种孝道出自人性中天然的本能，即便是面对冷酷无情的父母及兄弟，舜依然秉承着孝道的本真。

张博 制

9.2

万章问曰："《诗》云：'娶妻如之何？必告父母。'信斯言也，宜莫如舜。舜之不告而娶，何也？"

孟子曰："告则不得娶。男女居室，人之大伦也。如告，则废人之大伦，以怼[1]父母，是以不告也。"

万章曰："舜之不告而娶，则吾既得闻命矣。帝之妻舜而不告，何也？"

曰："帝亦知告焉则不得妻也。"

万章曰："父母使舜完廪，捐阶，瞽瞍焚廪。使浚井，出，从而掩之。象[2]曰：'谟盖[3]都君咸我绩。牛羊父母，仓廪父母，干戈朕，琴朕，弤[4]朕，二嫂使治朕栖[5]。'象往入舜宫，舜在床琴。象曰：'郁陶[6]思君尔。'忸怩。舜曰：'惟兹臣庶，汝其于予治。'不识舜不知象之将杀己与？"

曰："奚而不知也？象忧亦忧，象喜亦喜。"

曰："然则舜伪喜者与？"

曰："否。昔者有馈生鱼于郑子产，子产使校人[7]畜之池。校人烹之，反命曰：'始舍之圉圉[8]焉，少则洋洋[9]焉，攸然而逝。'子产曰：'得其所哉！得其所哉！'校人出，曰：'孰谓子产智？予既烹而食之，曰：得其所哉，得其所哉。'故君子可欺以其方[10]，难罔[11]以非其道。彼以爱兄之道来，故诚信而喜之，奚伪焉？"

Wan Zhang asked Mencius, saying, "It is said in the *Book of Poetry*, 'In marrying a wife, how ought a man to proceed? He must inform his parents.' If the rule be indeed as here expressed, no man ought to have illustrated it so well as Shun. How was it that Shun's marriage took place without his informing his parents?"

Mencius replied, "If he had informed them, he would not have been able to marry. That male and female should dwell together, is the greatest of human relations. If Shun had informed his parents, he must have made void this greatest of human relations, thereby incurring their resentment. On this account, he did not inform them!"

Wan Zhang said, "As to Shun's marrying without informing his parents, I have heard your instructions; but how was it that the emperor Yao gave him his daughters as wives without informing Shun's parents?"

Mencius said, "The emperor also knew that if he informed them, he could not marry his daughters to him."

Wan Zhang said, "His parents set Shun to repair a granary, to which, the ladder having been removed, Gusou set fire. They also made him dig a well. He got out, but they, not knowing that, proceeded to cover him up. Xiang said, 'Of the scheme to cover up the city-forming prince, the merit is all mine. Let my parents have his oxen and sheep. Let them have his storehouses and granaries. His shield and spear shall be mine. His lute shall be mine. His bow shall be mine. His two wives I shall make attend for me to my bed. ' Xiang then went away into Shun's palace, and there was Shun on his couch playing on his lute. Xiang said, 'I am coming simply because I was thinking anxiously about you.' At the same time, he blushed deeply. Shun said to him. 'There are all my officers: —do you undertake the government of them for me.' I do not know whether Shun was ignorant of Xiang's wishing to kill him."

Mencius answered, "How could he be ignorant of that? But when Xiang was sorrowful, he was also sorrowful; when Xiang was joyful, he was also joyful."

Wan Zhang said, "In that case, then, did not Shun rejoice hypocritically?"

Mencius replied, "No. Formerly, some one sent a present of a live fish to Zichan of Zhang. Zichan ordered his pond-keeper to keep it in the pond, but that officer cooked it, and reported the execution of his commission, saying, 'When I first let it go, it embarrassed. In a little while, it seemed to be somewhat at ease, then it swam away joyfully.' Zi-chan observed, 'It had got into its element! It had got into its element!' The pond-keeper then went out and said, 'Who calls Zichan a wise man? After I had cooked and eaten the fish, he said, It had got into its element! It had got into its element!' Thus a superior man may be imposed on by what seems to be as it ought to be, but he cannot be entrapped by what is contrary to right principle. Xiang came in the way in which the love of his elder brother would have made him come; therefore Shun sincerely believed him, and rejoiced. What hypocrisy was there?"

【注释】[1]怼(duì):怨恨。[2]象:人名,相传是舜的同父异母弟。[3]谟盖:谋害。谟:通“谋”。盖:通“害”。[4]弤(dǐ):舜弓之名。[5]栖:床。[6]郁陶(yáo):想念的样子。[7]校人:管理池塘的小官。[8]圉(yǔ)圉:气息奄奄的样子。[9]洋洋:舒缓摇尾的样子。[10]方:合乎情理的方法。[11]罔:诳骗,蒙蔽。

【译文】万章问道:“《诗经》上说:‘娶妻应该怎么办?一定要事先禀告自己的父母。’信从这句话的,应该没人比得上舜。但舜没有禀告父母就娶妻了,这是为什么呢?”

孟子说:“舜若禀告了父母便无法娶妻了。男女成婚,是很重要的人伦关系。若禀告了父母,就会破坏这重要的人伦关系,以至于怨恨父母,所以便不禀告了。”

万章说:“舜没有禀告父母便娶妻的道理,我已经懂得了。帝尧将女儿嫁给舜也没有告诉舜的父母，这又是为什么呢？”

（孟子）说：“尧帝也知道如果告诉了舜的父母，就不能把女儿嫁给舜了。”

万章说：“父母让舜去修补米仓，等舜上了屋顶，舜的父亲将梯子抽去，放火烧米仓。父母又让舜去淘井，不等舜出来，便往井里填土。舜的弟弟象说：‘谋害舜的计策都是我的功劳，牛羊归父母，仓廪归父母，干戈归我，琴归我，弓归我，两位嫂嫂为我铺床叠被。’象走入舜的房间，舜却坐在床边抚琴。象说：‘我非常想念你啊。’他的脸上显露出惭愧之色。舜说：‘我一心想的唯有臣子和百姓，你就协助我治理吧。’我不明白，舜难道不知道象要杀害他吗？”

（孟子）说：“怎么不知道？只不过象忧虑，他也忧虑；象高兴，他也高兴。”

（万章）说：“那么舜的高兴是假装的吗？”

（孟子）说：“不是。以前有人将一条

鱼送给郑国的子产，子产便让管理池塘的小吏养在池子里，小吏却把鱼煮来吃了，回来还说：‘刚开始把鱼放进池塘里，鱼还蔫蔫的，过了一会儿便游动自如了，（最后）突然迅速游远，不知去向了。’子产说：‘它去了它应该去的地方了！它去了它应该去的地方了！’小吏从子产那里出来后说：‘谁说子产聪明呢？我明明已经把鱼煮来吃了，可他还说：它去了它应该去的地方了！它去了它应该去的地方了！’所以，君子可能被合乎情理的方法所欺骗，但难以被不合情理的方法所欺骗。象假装一副敬爱兄长的样子，所以舜便诚心诚意地相信并为之高兴，怎么是假装的呢？”

【解读】孟子在本章告诉我们，舜不但恪守孝道，还是一位人伦的守护者，同时更是无与伦比的仁者。关于舜的家人置舜于死地而后快的故事，后世《史记·五帝本纪》中也有相同的记载，面对父母、兄弟的谋害，舜以自己特有的宽容、忍耐、善良和真诚去感化父母与兄弟。更为关键的是，舜的仁慈是发自于内心、顺从本性的，这既是孟子为舜辩解的着力点，也是“性善论”的有力支撑点。

孟子力图以舜的仁之大爱，树立仁人的楷模，弘扬儒家的仁者爱人的博爱精神，以减少家庭乃至整个社会的矛盾，建立和谐有序的家庭环境、社会环境。但就当今社会而言，舜的行为也并非全都可取，对谋财害命犯罪的一再纵容，可能会导致其更加疯狂，最终酿成大祸，故孟子在本章的辩解也有牵强之处，今人当有所取舍。

9.3

万章问曰："象日以杀舜为事，立为天子，则放之，何也？"

孟子曰："封之也，或曰放焉。"

万章曰："舜流共工[1]于幽州，放驩兜[2]于崇山，杀三苗[3]于三危，殛[4]鲧[5]于羽山，四罪而天下咸服，诛不仁也。象至不仁，封之有庳[6]。有庳之人奚罪焉？仁人固如是乎？在他人则诛之，在弟则封之？"

曰："仁人之于弟也，不藏怒焉，不宿怨焉，亲爱之而已矣。亲之，欲其贵也；爱之，欲其富也。封之有庳，富贵之也。身为天子，弟为匹夫，可谓亲爱之乎？"

"敢问或曰放者，何谓也？"

曰："象不得有为于其国，天子使吏治其国而纳其贡税焉，故谓之放。岂得暴彼民哉？虽然，欲常常而见之，故源源而来。'不及贡，以政接于有庳'，此之谓也。"

Wan Zhang said, "Xiang made it his daily business to slay Shun. When Shun was made sovereign, how was it that he only banished him?"

Mencius said, "He raised him to be a prince. Some supposed that it was banishing him?"

Wan Zhang said, "Shun banished the superintendent of works to Youzhou; he sent away Huandou to the mountain Chong; he slew the prince of San Miao in Sanwei; and he imprisoned Gun on the mountain Yu. When the crimes of those four were thus punished, the whole kingdom acquiesced: —it was a cutting off of men who were destitute of benevolence. But Xiang was of all men the most destitute of benevolence, and Shun raised him to be the prince of Youbi; —of what crimes had the people of Youbi been guilty? Does a benevolent man really act thus? In the case of other men, he cut them off; in the case of his brother, he raised him to be a prince."

Mencius replied, "A benevolent man does not

lay up anger, nor cherish resentment against his brother, but only regards him with affection and love. Regarding him with affection, he wishes him to be honourable; regarding him with love, he wishes him to be rich. The appointment of Xiang to be the prince of Youbi was to enrich and ennoble him. If while Shun himself was sovereign, his brother had been a common man, could he have been said to regard him with affection and love?"

Wan Zhang said, "I venture to ask what you mean by saying that some supposed that it was a banishing of Xiang?"

Mencius replied, "Xiang could do nothing in his state. The Son of Heaven appointed an officer to administer its government, and to pay over its revenues to him. This treatment of him led to its being said that he was banished. How indeed could he be allowed the means of oppressing the people? Nevertheless, Shun wished to be continually seeing him, and by this arrangement, he came incessantly to court, as is signified in that expression: — 'He did not wait for the rendering of tribute, or affairs of government, to receive the prince of Youbi.' "

【注释】［1］共工：相传为尧的大臣。［2］驩（huān）兜：相传是尧、舜时的大臣，三苗族的首领。［3］三苗：国名。［4］殛（jí）：杀。［5］鲧（gǔn）：传说是禹的父亲，尧曾派他治水，但没有成功。［6］有庳（bì）：国名，传说是象的封地。

【译文】万章问道："象天天都把谋杀舜当作自己要干的事，舜做了天子后，只是流放了他，这是为什么？"

孟子说："其实是舜封象为诸侯，不过有人说是流放他罢了。"

万章说："舜把共工流放到幽州，把驩兜发配到崇山，在三危诛杀三苗的君主，在

羽山处决了鲧，四次治罪举措使得天下都归服，因为惩处的是不仁之人。象是最不仁的人，却封给他有庳，有庳的百姓有什么罪呢？对旁人，就严加治罪；对弟弟，就封他诸侯，难道仁人的做法都是如此吗？”

（孟子）说：“仁人对于自己的弟弟，不藏怒气在心里，不留怨恨在胸中，只知道要亲近他、爱护他罢了。亲近他，就想让他尊贵；爱护他，就想让他富有。把有庳封给他，就是要让他既富有又尊贵。自己当了天子，弟弟却是一个平民百姓，能说是亲近他、爱护他吗？”

（万章又问道：）“我想请问，为什么有人说是流放呢？”

（孟子）说：“象不能够直接管理国家，天子派了官吏去治理他的国家并缴纳贡税，所以有人说是流放。怎能让他对百姓施行暴政呢？虽然这样，舜还想常常见到象，所以象不断地来和舜相见。（古书上说）‘不必等到朝贡的日子，平常就以政事为名接见有庳的国君’，就是说的这种情况。”

【解读】本章孟子提出了“亲亲”的合理性，这种合理性是建立在“仁人”的基础之上，既继承了孔子“仁者爱人”的学说，又发展了儒家“亲亲相隐”的理论。通过象的不仁不义，与舜的大仁大义形成鲜明对比，通过对共工、驩兜、三苗的君主及鲧四位违背天命的失败者、危及公共利益者的处罚，与象的处理结果进行比照，凸显了舜胸怀天下的仁德。

在今天看来，“亲亲”是一种偏私行为，有失公允，但在古人那里却有着天然的合理成分，并认为是一种“仁人”的表现。成语“藏怒宿怨”出自本章，意指把愤怒和怨恨藏留在心里，久久难消。“不藏怒焉，不宿怨焉”则是一种完全出自天生善性的做法。所以，孟子在此肯定舜封象的举动，这是针对当时人伦丧失、杀兄弑父的上层社会现实做出的有力回应。

9.4

咸丘蒙[1]问曰："语云：'盛德之士，君不得而臣，父不得而子。'舜南面而立，尧帅诸侯北面而朝之，瞽瞍亦北面而朝之。舜见瞽瞍，其容有蹙[2]。孔子曰：'于斯时也，天下殆哉，岌岌乎！'不识此语诚然乎哉？"

孟子曰："否，此非君子之言，齐东野人之语也。尧老而舜摄也。《尧典》曰：'二十有八载，放勋乃徂落[3]，百姓如丧考妣[4]，三年，四海遏密八音[5]。'孔子曰：'天无二日，民无二王。'舜既为天子矣，又帅天下诸侯以为尧三年丧，是二天子矣。"

咸丘蒙曰："舜之不臣尧，则吾既得闻命矣。《诗》云：'普天之下，莫非王土；率土之滨，莫非王臣。'而舜既为天子矣，敢问瞽瞍之非臣，如何？"

曰："是诗也，非是之谓也；劳于王事而不得养父母也。曰：'此莫非王事，我独贤劳也。’故说诗者，不以文害辞，不以辞害志。以意逆志，是为得之。如以辞而已矣，《云汉》之诗曰：‘周余黎民，靡有孑遗[6]。’信斯言也，是周无遗民也。孝子之至，莫大乎尊亲；尊亲之至，莫大乎以天下养。为天子父，尊之至也；以天下养，养之至也。《诗》曰：‘永言孝思，孝思维则[7]。’此之谓也。《书》曰：‘祗载见瞽瞍，夔夔齐栗[8]，瞽瞍亦允若。’是为父不得而子也？”

Xianqiu Meng asked Mencius, saying, “There is the saying, ‘A scholar of complete virtue may not be employed as a minister by his sovereign, nor treated as a son by his father. Shun stood with his face to the south, and Yao, at the head of all the princes, appeared before him at court with his face to the north. Gusou also did the same. When Shun saw Gusou, his countenance became discomposed. Confucius said, ‘At this time, in what a perilous condition was the kingdom! Its state was indeed unsettled.' —I do not know whether what is here said really took place."

Mencius replied, "No. These are not the words of a superior man. They are the sayings of an uncultivated person of the east of Qi. When Yao was old, Shun was associated with him in the government. It is said in the *Canon of Yao*, 'After twenty and eight years, the Highly Meritorious one deceased. The people acted as if they were mourning for a father or mother for three years, and up to the borders of the four seas every sound of music was hushed. ' Confucius said, 'There are not two suns in the sky, nor two sovereigns over the people.' Shun having been sovereign, and, moreover, leading on all the princes to observe the three years' mourning for Yao, there would have been in this case two sovereigns."

Xianqiu Meng said, "On the point of Shun's

not treating Yao as a minister, I have received your instructions. But it is said in the *Book of Poetry*, 'Under the whole heaven, every spot is the sovereign's ground; to the borders of the land, every individual is the sovereign's minister.' —And Shun had become sovereign. I venture to ask how it was that Gusou was not one of his ministers."

Mencius answered, "That ode is not to be understood in that way: —It speaks of being laboriously engaged in the sovereign's business, so as not to be able to nourish one's parents, as if the author said, 'This is all the sovereign's business, and how is it that I alone am supposed to have ability, and am made to toil in it?' Therefore, those who explain the odes, may not insist on one term so as to do violence to a sentence, nor on a sentence so as to do violence to the general scope. They must try with their thoughts to meet that scope, and then we shall apprehend it. If we simply take single

sentences, there is that in the ode called *The Milky Way*, —'Of the black-haired people of the remnant of Zhou, There is not half a one left.' If it had been really as thus expressed, then not an individual of the people of Zhou was left. Of all which a filial son can attain to, there is nothing greater than his honouring his parents. And of what can be attained to in the honouring one's parents, there is nothing greater than the nourishing them with the whole kingdom. Gusou was the father of the sovereign; — this was the height of honour. Shun nourished him with the whole kingdom; —this was the height of nourishing. In this was verified the sentiment in the *Book of Poetry*, 'Ever cherishing filial thoughts, those filial thoughts became an example to after ages.' It is said in the *Book of History*, 'Reverently performing his duties, he waited on Gusou, and was full of veneration and awe. Gusou also believed him and conformed to virtue.' This is the true case of the scholar of complete virtue not being treated as a son by his father."

【注释】［1］咸丘蒙：姓咸丘，名蒙，孟子弟子。［2］蹙（cù）：不安。［3］徂（cú）落：同"殂落"，死亡。［4］考妣（bǐ）：父母。［5］八音：中国古代对乐器的统称，指金、石、土、革、丝、木、匏、竹八种材料制成的乐器。这里指代音乐。［6］孑（jié）遗：遗留。［7］维则：作为行动的原则。［8］夔（kuí）夔齐栗：因谨慎而战栗的样子。

【译文】咸丘蒙问道："古语说：'很有道德的人，君主不能以他为臣，父亲不能以他为子。'舜南面而立做了天子，尧率领诸侯朝见他，他父亲瞽瞍也朝见他。舜见了瞽瞍，容貌局促不安。孔子说：'在这个时候呀，天下真是危险到极点了！'不知这句话真是如此的吗？"

孟子说："不，这不是君子说的话，是齐国东边乡下人说的话。尧老了，舜代行天子职权。《尧典》上说：'（舜代行天子职权）二十八年，尧才去世，群臣如同死了父母一般，服丧三年，天下不闻音乐之声。'孔子说：'天上没有两个太阳，人间没有两个帝王。'如果舜在尧死之前真做了天子，又率领天下诸侯为尧服丧三年，这就同时有两个天子了。"

咸丘蒙说："舜没有把尧当作臣，我已领受了您的教诲了。《诗经》上说：'普天之下，没有哪里不是天子的土地；四海之内，没有一人不是天子的臣民。'舜已经做了天子了，瞽瞍却不是他的臣民，请问这又是怎么回事？"

（孟子）说："这首诗，不是说的这个意思；而是说公事劳碌以致不能奉养父母。（意思是）说：'这些没有一件不是公事，却只有我最劳碌。'所以解说诗经的人，不要拘于文字而误解言辞，也不要拘于言辞而误解作者的本意。要用自己的思考来领会诗意，这样才能把握住诗的真谛。如果只拘泥于言辞，那么《云汉》这首诗说过：‘周朝剩下的百姓，没有一个存留。’相信了这句话，这就成了周朝没有一个人留存了。孝子的最高境界，莫过于尊敬自己的父母；尊敬父母的最高境界，莫过于用天下奉养父母。作为天子的父亲，这是最尊贵的地位了；用天下奉养父亲，这是最高的奉养了。《诗经》上说：‘永远行孝道，孝道就是法则。’说的就是这个意思。《尚书》上说：‘舜恭恭敬敬地去见瞽瞍，谨慎而又畏惧，瞽瞍也就真的顺心了。’这是‘父亲不能把他当儿子’吗？”

【解读】本章仍旧讨论舜帝。咸丘蒙转述了一个有关舜帝的传言，即舜为天子之后，尧帝与瞽瞍都去朝见他，并询问是怎样一回事。孟子认为这是齐东乡下人乱讲的，尧去世之前，舜不过是摄政，而不是天子，所以尧朝见舜是谣言。而对于后者，弟子咸丘蒙仍紧紧追问，并引用《诗》中语句“普天之下，莫非王土；率土之滨，莫非王臣”作为凭据。孟子认为舜虽然成为天子，但仍旧是瞽瞍的儿子，二者仍以父子关系相处，至于所提到的“莫非王臣”，实际是咸丘蒙曲解了本义。孟子还指出了舜的至孝，即“尊亲”与“天下养”。“天下养”是我们常人无法做到的，但“尊亲”人人可为，尊重父母的兴趣、习惯与选择，才是孝道的首要原则。除此之外，本章孟子针对读诗所提出的“不以文害辞，不以辞害志”与“以意逆志”，在中国古代文学批评中产生了极为深刻的影响，在一定程度上也反过来影响了中国诗歌的创作理念。

9.5

万章曰："尧以天下与舜，有诸？"

孟子曰："否。天子不能以天下与人。"

"然则舜有天下也，孰与之？"

曰："天与之。"

"天与之者，谆谆[1]然命之乎？"

曰："否。天不言，以行与事示之而已矣。"

曰："以行与事示之者，如之何？"

曰："天子能荐人于天，不能使天与之天下；诸侯能荐人于天子，不能使天子与之诸侯；大夫能荐人于诸侯，不能使诸侯与之大夫。昔者，尧荐舜于天，而天受之；暴[2]之于民，而民受之。故曰：天不言，以行与事示之而已矣。"

曰："敢问荐之于天，而天受之；暴之于民，而民受之，如何？"

曰："使之主祭而百神享之，是天受之；使之主事而事治，百姓安之，是民受之也。

天与之，人与之，故曰：天子不能以天下与人。舜相尧二十有八载，非人之所能为也，天也。尧崩，三年之丧毕，舜避尧之子于南河[3]之南，天下诸侯朝觐者，不之尧之子而之舜；讼狱[4]者，不之尧之子而之舜；讴歌者，不讴歌尧之子而讴歌舜，故曰天也。夫然后之中国[5]，践天子位焉。而[6]居尧之宫，逼尧之子，是篡也，非天与也。《太誓》曰‘天视自我民视，天听自我民听’，此之谓也。”

Wan Zhang said, “Was it the case that Yao gave the throne to Shun?”

Mencius said, “No. The sovereign cannot give the throne to another.”

“Yes; —but Shun had the throne. Who gave it to him?”

“Heaven gave it to him,” was the answer.

“ ‘Heaven gave it to him’, did Heaven confer its appointment on him with specific injunctions?”

Mencius replied, "No. Heaven does not speak. It simply showed its will by his personal conduct and his conduct of affairs."

Wan Zhang, " 'It showed its will by his personal conduct and his conduct of affairs' —how was this?"

Mencius's answer was, "The sovereign can present a man to Heaven, but he cannot make Heaven give that man the throne. A prince can present a man to the sovereign, but he cannot cause the sovereign to make that man a prince. A great officer can present a man to his prince, but he cannot cause the prince to make that man a great officer. Yao presented Shun to Heaven, and Heaven accepted him. He presented him to the people, and the people accepted him. Therefore I say, 'Heaven does not speak. It simply indicated its will by his personal conduct and his conduct of affairs.' "

Wan Zhang said, "I presume to ask how it was that Yao presented Shun to Heaven, and Heaven accepted him; and that he exhibited him to the people, and the people accepted him."

Mencius replied, "He caused him to preside over the sacrifices, and all the spirits were well pleased with them; —thus Heaven accepted him. He caused him to preside over the conduct of affairs, and affairs were well administered, so that the people reposed under him; —thus the people accepted him. Heaven gave the throne to him. The people gave it to him. Therefore I said, 'The sovereign cannot give the throne to another.' Shun assisted Yao in the government for twenty and eight years; —this was more than man could have done, and was from Heaven. After the death of Yao, when the three years' mourning was completed, Shun withdrew from the son of Yao to the south of South River. The princes of the kingdom, however, repairing to court, went not to the son of Yao, but they went to Shun. Litigants went not to the son of Yao, but they went to Shun. Singers sang not the son of Yao, but they sang Shun. Therefore I said, 'Heaven gave him the throne.' It was after these things that he went to the Middle Kingdom, and occupied the seat of the Son of Heaven. If he had, before these things, taken up his residence in the palace of Yao, and had applied pressure to the son of Yao, it would have been an act of usurpation, and not the gift of Heaven. This sentiment is expressed in the words of the *Great Declaration*: — 'Heaven sees according as my people see; Heaven hears according as my people hear.' "

【注释】［1］谆谆（zhūn）：教导不倦，反复告诫。［2］暴（pù）：显露，公布。［3］南河：即黄河，因在尧都的南面，故称。［4］讼狱：因断案不明而争论是非曲直。［5］中国：这里指国家的都城。［6］而：如果。

【译文】万章问道："尧把天下授予舜，有这回事吗？”

孟子说：“没有。天子不能把天下授予人。”

（万章又问：）“那么，舜拥有的天下是谁授予的呢？”

（孟子）说：“天授予的。”

（万章问：）“天授予的，是反复叮咛告诫他的吗？”

（孟子）说：“不是。天不说话，凭舜的行动和能力表明是天给了他天下罢了。”

（万章）问：“凭舜的行动和能力表明天给了他天下，这怎么说？”

（孟子）说：“天子能把人推荐给天，却不能让天把天下给这个人；诸侯能把人推荐给天子，却不能让天子把诸侯的职位给这个人；大夫能把人推荐给诸侯，却不能让诸侯把大夫的职位给这个人。从前，尧把舜推荐给天，天接受了；把舜介绍给百姓，百姓接受了。所以说，天不说话，凭舜的行为和事实表明把天下给了他罢了。”

（万章）问：“请问，把舜推荐给天，天接受了；把舜介绍给百姓，百姓也接受了，这是怎样的呢？”

（孟子）说：“派舜主持祭祀，百神都来享用祭品，这表明天接受了他；派舜主持政事，政事办得妥帖，百姓对他放心，这表明百姓接受了他。天授给他，百姓授给他，所以说，天子不能把天下送给他人。舜帮助尧治理天下二十八年，这不是人的意愿所能决定的，而是天的旨意。尧去世了，三年服丧结束，舜避开尧的儿子，到了南河的南面，（但是）天下诸侯来朝见天子，却不到尧的儿子那里去，而到舜那里去；打官司的，不到尧的儿子那里去，而到舜那里去；讴歌的人，不讴歌尧的儿子，而讴歌舜，所以说，这是天的旨意。舜这才回到国都，登上了天子的位子。（假如他当初）搬进尧的宫室，逼迫尧的儿子让位，这就是篡位了，不是天授给他的了。《尚书·泰誓》上说过，‘天的看法来自我们百姓的看法，天的听闻来自我们百姓的听闻’，说的就是这个意思。”

【解读】本章在说明君权天授的同时，更强调“民受”，“民受”决定“天与”，这就是先秦儒家所谓“君权天与，天权民授”的学说。这里是说，禅让天下并不是个人的意愿所决定的，候选人的行为与能力必须合乎上天的选择标准，而且还要看民众是否接受。直白地说就是“民意”“天意”的直接表现和合法代表。

所谓的“天与之”“民与之”，即是权力公有，既要得到上天的授权，还要得到民众的拥护，这里体现出孟子天下为公的思想。想要得到百姓真心拥护，执政者必须有相当的执政能力，为百姓谋福祉，正因为舜达到“使之主事而事治，百姓安之，是民受之也”的程度，故“天下诸侯朝觐者，不之尧之子

孟子与万章讨论问题　韩维新 绘

而之舜；讼狱者，不之尧之子而之舜；讴歌者，不讴歌尧之子而讴歌舜”，舜自然而然成为天子。最后，孟子引用《尚书》中的“天视自我民视，天听自我民听”来告诫当权者，权位虽是“天与”，但追其本源还是“民受”。孟子此番言论，既是对篡权贼子的理论颠覆与行为批判，也是“仁政”思想的一种阐发，体现了我国先秦时代朴素的“民本”思想。

9.6

万章问曰："人有言：'至于禹而德衰，不传于贤而传于子。'有诸？"

孟子曰："否，不然也。天与贤，则与贤；天与子，则与子。昔者舜荐禹于天，十有七年，舜崩。三年之丧毕，禹避舜之子于阳城[1]。天下之民从之，若尧崩之后，不从尧之子而从舜也。禹荐益[2]于天，七年，禹崩。三年之丧毕，益避禹之子于箕山[3]之阴。朝觐讼狱者不之益而之启，曰：'吾君之子也。'讴歌者不讴歌益而讴歌启，曰：'吾君之子也。'丹朱[4]之不肖，舜之子亦不肖。舜之相尧、禹之相舜也，历年多，施泽于民久。启贤，能敬承继禹之道。益之相禹也，历年少，施泽于民未久。舜、禹、益相去久远，其子之贤不肖，皆天也，非人之所能为也。莫之为而为者，天也；莫之致而至者，命也。匹夫而有天下者，德必若舜、禹，而又有天子荐之者，

故仲尼不有天下。继世以有天下，天之所废，必若桀、纣者也，故益、伊尹、周公不有天下。伊尹相汤以王于天下，汤崩，太丁[5]未立，外丙[6]二年，仲壬四年。太甲[7]颠覆汤之典刑，伊尹放之于桐[8]。三年，太甲悔过，自怨自艾，于桐处仁迁义。三年，以听伊尹之训己也，复归于亳[9]。周公之不有天下，犹益之于夏、伊尹之于殷也。孔子曰：'唐、虞[10]禅，夏后殷、周继，其义一也。'"

Wan Zhang asked Mencius, saying, "People say, 'When the disposal of the kingdom came to Yu, his virtue was inferior to that of Yao and Shun, and he transmitted it not to the worthiest but to his son.' Was it so?"

Mencius replied, "No; it was not so. When Heaven gave the kingdom to the worthiest, it was given to the worthiest. When Heaven gave it to the son of the preceding sovereign, it was given to him.

Shun presented Yu to Heaven. Seventeen years elapsed, and Shun died. When the three years' mourning was expired, Yu withdrew from the son of Shun to Yang Cheng. The people of the kingdom followed him just as after the death of Yao, instead of following his son, they had followed Shun. Yu presented Yi to Heaven. Seven years elapsed, and Yu died. When the three years' mourning was expired, Yi withdrew from the son of Yu to the north of mount Qi. The princes, repairing to court, went not to Yi, but they went to Qi. Litigants did not go to Yi, but they went to Qi, saying, 'He is the son of our sovereign;' the singers did not sing Yi, but they sang Qi, saying, 'He is the son of our sovereign.' That Danzhu was not equal to his father, and Shun's son not equal to his; that Shun assisted Yao, and Yu assisted Shun, for many years, conferring benefits on the people for a long time; that thus the length of time during which Shun, Yu, and Yi assisted in the government was so different; that Qi was able, as a man of talents and virtue, reverently to pursue the same course as Yu; that Yi assisted Yu only for a few years, and had not long conferred benefits on the people; that the periods of service of the three were so different; and that the sons were one superior and the other superior: —all this was from Heaven, and what could not be brought about by man. That which is done without man's doing is from Heaven. That which happens withont man's causing is from the ordinance of Heaven. In the case of a private individual obtaining the throne, there must be in him virtue equal to that of Shun or Yu; and moreover there must be the presenting of him to Heaven by the preceding sovereign. It was on this account that Confucius did not obtain the throne. When the kingdom is possessed by natural succession, the sovereign who is displaced by Heaven must be like Jie or Zhou. It was on this account that Yi, Yi

Yin, and Zhou Gong did not obtain the throne. Yi Yin assisted Tang so that he became sovereign over the kingdom. After the demise of Tang, Taiding having died before he could be appointed sovereign, Waibing reigned two years, and Zhongren four. Tai Jia was then turning upside down the statutes of Tang, when Yi Yin placed him in Tong for three years. There Tai Jia repented of his errors, was contrite, and reformed himself. In Tong he came to dwell in benevolence and walk in righteousness, during those three years, listening to the lessons given to him by Yi Yin. Then Yi Yin again returned with him to Bo. Zhougong not getting the throne was like the case of Yi and the throne of Xia, or like that of Yi Yin and the throne of Yin. Confucius said, 'Tang and Yu resigned the throne to their worthy ministers. The sovereign of Xia and those of Yin and Zhou transmitted it to their sons. The principle of righteousness was the same in all the cases.' "

【注释】[1]阳城：地名，在今河南登封东南。[2]益：古代嬴姓各族的祖先，因助禹治水有功，被选为继承人。[3]箕山：在今河南登封东南。[4]丹朱：传说中尧之子，名朱，因居丹水，名为丹朱。传说他傲慢荒淫，尧因此禅位给舜。[5]太丁：汤的长子。[6]外丙：太丁的弟弟。下句仲壬是外丙的弟弟。[7]太甲：汤的嫡长孙，太丁之子。[8]桐：地名，在今河南偃师县西南，一说在山西荣河县。[9]亳(bó)：地名，商汤的国都，在今河南偃师县西。[10]唐虞：相传尧建立的朝代叫“唐”，舜建立的朝代叫“虞”。

【译文】万章问道：“人们有这样的说法：‘到了禹的时候道德就衰微了，（帝位）不传给贤人却传给自己的儿子。’有这事吗？”

孟子说：“不，不是这样的。天要传给贤人，就传给贤人；天要传给君主的儿子，就传给君主的儿子。从前，舜把禹推荐给天，十七年后，舜去世了。三年丧期完后，禹避开舜的儿子到阳城，天下百姓都跟随着他，就像尧去世后，百姓不跟随尧的儿子却跟随舜一样。禹把益推荐给天，七年后，禹去世了，三年丧期完后，益避开禹的儿子到了箕山北面。来朝见的诸侯及打官司的人不到益那里去，而到启那里去，说：‘（他是）我们君主的儿子。’讴歌的人不讴歌益而讴歌启，说：‘（他是）我们君主的儿子。’（尧的儿子）丹朱不成器，舜的儿子也不成器。舜辅佐尧、禹辅佐舜，经历了很多年，施给百姓恩泽的时间也长。启很贤明，能恭敬地继承禹的做法。益辅佐禹的年数少，施给百姓恩泽的时间不长。舜、禹、益之间相距的时间有长有短，他们的儿子有好有坏，这都出自天意，不是人的意愿所能决定的。凡事不是人力所能及的却自然而成的，都是天意；不是人力招致它来却自然而然地来到了，这是命运。一个普通百姓却能得到天下，他的

德性必然像舜和禹那样，而且还要有天子推荐他，所以仲尼（虽然圣贤，但没有天子推荐）不能够得到天下。世代相传而得到了天下的，天意如要让他丧失天下，必然是像桀、纣那样残暴无德的君主，所以益、伊尹、周公（虽然圣贤，但他们所辅佐的不是桀、纣那样的君主）就不能够得到天下。伊尹辅佐汤称王天下，汤死后，太丁没有继位（就死了），外丙在位两年，仲壬在位四年。太甲（继位后）破坏了汤的典章法度，伊尹把他流放到桐邑。三年后，太甲悔过，怨恨自己，改正自己，在桐邑做到心不离仁，行合乎义。三年后，已能听从伊尹的训导了，才又回到亳都（做天子）。周公不能得到天下（的原因），正如同益处在夏朝、伊尹处在殷朝一样。孔子说：'唐尧、虞舜让位给贤人，夏、商、周三代由子孙继位，其中的道理是相通的。'"

【解读】本章主要讨论王朝继承的问题。上古时代，大部落首领多由推举产生，以禅让的方式实现继承人的更迭，例如尧传之舜，舜传之禹。而到了禹，却传给了他的儿子启，从此由“公天下”变为“家天下”，所以一些人便认为“至于禹而德衰”。孟子不认同这个观点，他将最高统治者的更迭归结于天意与命运，在此基础上，以仲尼、益、伊尹、周公为典例解释了尧、舜让贤和夏商周由子孙继位的原因。

孟子将最高统治者的继承归结于天意与命运，以唯物史观来看，无疑是站不住脚的，这也是孟子自身思想的局限所在；但继承人是否具备资格，是以民心向背为外在表现，这就将民意在一定意义上等同为天意，以此来建立民意的权威。而要取得这一资格，须得具备“德”，故继承人的考量仍是以“德”为内在标尺。孟子通过对这一概念的转化，将历史的偶然性与必然性进行了有机统一，给当时的统治者敲响警钟的同时，也构造了

“王天下”的蓝图。

另外，孟子之所以与万章谈论这个问题，与当时的禅让思潮的兴起，特别是燕王哙地让国事件（燕王哙让国于子之，引发了社会动荡，最后落得身败名裂）有关，是具有一定时代背景的，故我们对于本章的理解也应当回归于历史语境，只有这样，才能够理解孟子提出天意与命运的考虑。

9.7

万章问曰："人有言'伊尹以割烹要[1]汤'有诸？"

孟子曰："否，不然。伊尹耕于有莘之野，而乐尧、舜之道焉。非其义也，非其道也，禄之以天下，弗顾也；系马千驷，弗视也。非其义也，非其道也，一介不以与人，一介不以取诸人。汤使人以币聘之，嚣嚣然[2]曰：'我何以汤之聘币为哉？我岂若处畎亩之中，由是以乐尧、舜之道哉？'汤三使往聘之，既而幡然[3]改曰：'与我处畎亩之中，由是以乐尧、舜之道，吾岂若使是君为尧、舜之君哉？吾岂若使是民为尧、舜之民哉？吾岂若于吾身亲见之哉？天之生此民也，使先知觉[4]后知，使先觉觉后觉也。予，天民之先觉者也；予将以斯道觉斯民也。非予觉之，而谁也？'思天下之民匹夫匹妇有不被尧、舜之泽者，若己推而内[5]之沟中。其自任以天下之重如此，故就汤而说之以伐夏救民。吾未闻枉己而正人者也，况辱己以正天下者乎？圣人之行不同也，或远或近，或去或不去，归洁其身而已矣。吾闻其以尧、舜之道要汤，未闻以割烹也。《伊训》[6]曰：'天诛造攻[7]自牧宫[8]，朕载自亳[9]。'"

Wan Zhang asked Mencius, saying, "People say that Yi Yin sought an introduction to Tang by his knowledge of cookery. Was it so?"

Mencius replied, "No, it was not so. Yi Yin was a farmer in the lands of the prince of Xin, delighting in the principles of Yao and Shun. In any matter contrary to the righteousness which they prescribed, or contrary to their principles, though he had been offered the throne, he would not have regarded it; though there had been yoked for him a thousand teams of horses, he would not have looked at them. In any matter contrary to the righteousness which they prescribed, or contrary to their principles, he would neither have given nor taken a single straw. Tang sent persons with presents of silk to entreat him to enter his service. With an air of indifference and self-satisfaction he said, 'What can I do with those silks with which Tang invites me? Is it not best for me to abide in the channelled fields, and so delight myself with the principles of Yao and Shun?' Tang thrice sent messengers to invite him. After this, with the change of resolution displayed in his countenance, he spoke in a different style, — 'Instead of abiding in the channelled fields and thereby delighting myself with the principles of Yao and Shun, had I not better make this prince a prince like Yao or Shun, and this people like the people of Yao or Shun? Had I not better in my own person see these things for myself? Heaven's plan in the production of mankind is this: —that they who are first informed should instruct those who are later in being informed, and they who first apprehend principles should instruct those who are slower to do so. I am one of Heaven's people who have first apprehended; I will take these principles and instruct this people in them. If I do not instruct them, who will do so?' He thought that among all the people of the kingdom, even the private men and women, if there were any who did not enjoy such benefits as Yao and Shun conferred, it was as if he himself pushed them into a ditch. He took upon himself the heavy charge of the kingdom in this way, and therefore he went to Tang, and pressed upon him the subject of attacking Xia and saving the people. I have not heard of one who bent himself, and at the same time made others straight;—how much less could one disgrace himself,and thereby rectify the whole kingdom? The actions of the sages have been different. Some have kept remote from court, and some have drawn near to it; some have left their offices, and some have not done so: —that to which those different courses all agree is simply the keeping of their persons pure. I have heard that Yi Yin sought an introduction to Tang by the doctrines of Yao and Shun. I have not heard that he did so by his knowledge of cookery. In the *Instructions of Yi,* it is said, 'Heaven destroying Jie commenced attacking him in the palace of Mu. I commenced in Bo.' "

【注释】[1]要：求。[2]嚣嚣然：自得之志，无欲之貌。[3]幡然：形容迅速的样子。[4]觉：开悟，开导。[5]内：通"纳"，放进。[6]《伊训》：《尚书》篇名，已佚，今本《尚书》中该篇为伪古文。[7]造：作也。攻：讨也。[8]牧宫：桀的宫室，代指桀自身。[9]朕：我。先秦时期"朕"是一般的自称，秦始皇以后成为皇帝的专用自称。载：始也。亳：商都。

【译文】万章问道："有人说'伊尹通过割烹（当厨子）来求得汤给他官做'，有这事吗？"

孟子说："不，不是这样的。伊尹在有莘的荒远之地耕种，且乐于尧舜之道啊。不是尧舜之义，不是尧舜之道，以天下作为俸禄，他也不屑一顾；即使给他四千匹马，他也不会看一眼。不是尧舜之义，不是尧舜之道，一根草也不给别人，也不从别人那里拿一根草。汤使人拿礼品去聘请他，他却不以为然地说：'我要汤给的礼品做什么？怎么比得上我待在田地里，由此来乐享尧舜之道呢？'汤多次使人去聘请伊尹，接着伊尹突然间改变了最初的想法，说：'我待在田地里，独自乐于尧舜之道，怎么比得上我让君主成为尧舜之类的君主呢？怎么比得上我让民众成为尧舜时期的民众呢？怎么比得上（尧舜盛世）让我自己亲眼所见呢？天之所以生这些民众，是让先知道的人开导后知道的人，让先觉悟的人开导后觉悟的人啊。我，是天生之民里面先觉悟的人，我将用这个道来开导那些后觉悟的人啊。不是我来开悟他们，还能有谁呢？’想到天下的民众匹夫匹妇有得不到尧舜之道的恩泽的，就好像是自己把他们推进沟里一样。伊尹把天下的重任放在自己身上就是这般，所以就很高兴地去汤那里，通过攻伐夏桀来拯救万民。我没有听说过自己不正却能匡正别人的，何况侮辱自己却能匡正天下的呢？圣人的行为有所差异，有疏远君主的，有接近君主的；有离开朝廷的，有留在朝廷的，只不过最后都能做到身洁罢了。我只听说伊尹用尧舜之道向汤求官，没听说是通过割烹（当厨师）啊。《伊训》说：‘天要诛杀夏桀，祸端是从他自身开始的，而我只是从亳都开始谋划罢了。’”

【解读】孟子在本章通过伊尹前后的思想转变，赞扬了尧舜之道的同时，也赞誉了伊尹高尚的品质。伊尹原本甘于平凡，隐居于山野，以尧舜之道独善其身。后来，汤多次使人去聘请，伊尹觉悟到这种独善其身的修行对人世间的贡献不大，幡然悔悟，想要用尧舜之道使天下民众受益。伊尹作为一位先觉者，认为有责任和义务使君王成为尧舜之类的君王，使民众成为尧舜时期的民众，使天下成为类似尧舜时代的盛世。于是，伊尹选择出仕以求兼济天下，义不容辞地辅助商汤攻伐夏桀来拯救万民。

关于伊尹，《史记·殷本纪》记载有两种说法："伊尹名阿衡。阿衡欲奸汤而无由，乃为有莘氏媵臣，负鼎俎，以滋味说汤，致于王道。或曰，伊尹处士，汤使人聘迎之，五反然后肯往从汤，言素王及九主之事。"故而史有"伊尹以割烹要汤"之说，而孟子这里采信后者。孟子之所以崇拜伊尹，大概是他也想成为伊尹那样的人辅佐圣王之师，用"尧舜之道""尧舜之义"拯救天下。同时，孟子也从伊尹的行为中，明白了作为先觉者的使命。

9.8

万章问曰："或谓孔子于卫主痈疽[1]，于齐主侍人瘠环[2]，有诸乎？"

孟子曰："否，不然也。好事者为之也。于卫主颜雠由[3]。弥子[4]之妻与子路之妻，兄弟也。弥子谓子路曰：'孔子主我，卫卿可得也。'子路以告。孔子曰：'有命。'孔子进以礼，退以义，得之不得曰'有命'。而主痈疽与侍人瘠环，是无义无命也。孔子不悦于鲁、卫，遭宋桓司马[5]将要[6]而杀之，微服[7]而过宋。是时孔子当厄，主司城贞子[8]，为陈侯周[9]臣。吾闻观近臣[10]，以其所为主；观远臣[11]，以其所主。若孔子主痈疽与侍人瘠环，何以为孔子？"

Wan Zhang asked Mencius, saying, "Some say that Confucius, when he was in Wei, lived with the ulcer-doctor, and when he was in Qi, with the attendant, Ji Huan; —was it so?"

Mencius replied, "No; it was not so. Those are the inventions of men fond of strange things. When he was in Wei, he lived with Yan Chouyou. The wives of the officer Mi and Zilu were sisters, and Mi told Zilu, 'If Confucius will lodge with me, he may attain to the dignity of a high noble of Wei.' Zilu informed Confucius of this, and he said, 'That is as ordered by Heaven.' Confucius went into office according to propriety, and retired from it according to righteousness. In regard to his obtaining office or not obtaining it, he said, 'That is as ordered.' But if he had lodged with the attendant Ji Huan, that would neither have been according to righteousness, nor any ordering of Heaven. When Confucius, being dissatisfied in Lu and Wei, had left those states, he met with the attempt of Huan, the Master of the Horse, of Song, to intercept and kill him. He assumed, however, the dress of a common man, and passed by Song. At that time, though he was in circumstances of distress, he lodged with the city master Zheng, who was then a minister of Zhou, the marquis of Chen. I have heard that the characters of ministers about court may be discerned from those whom they entertain, and those of stranger officers, from those with whom they lodge. If Confucius had lodged with the ulcer-doctor, and with the attendant Ji Huan, how could he have been Confucius?"

【注释】[1]主痈疽(yōng jū):以痈疽为主人,指住在痈疽家里。痈疽:人名,卫灵公所宠信的宦官。[2]侍人:即"寺人",宦官。瘠环:人名,齐景公宠信的宦官。[3]颜雠由:卫国大夫,有贤名。[4]弥子:即弥子瑕,卫灵公的宠臣。[5]桓司马:即宋国的司马桓魋(tuí)。司马,官职名,掌管军政和军赋。[6]要(yāo):拦截。[7]微服:指变易平时的服装以避人耳目。[8]司城贞子:陈

国大夫。［9］陈侯周：陈怀公子，名周。［10］近臣：在朝之臣。［11］远臣：外来的臣。

【译文】万章问道："有人说孔子在卫国时寄住在宦官痈疽家里以痈疽为主人，在齐国时寄住在宦官瘠环家里以瘠环为主人，真有这回事吗？"

孟子说："不，不是这么回事。是好事者编造出来的。孔子在卫国寄住在颜雠由家。弥子瑕的妻子与子路的妻子是姊妹。弥子瑕曾对子路说：'孔子来住在我家，卫国卿相的位置就可以得到。'子路把这话告诉给孔子。孔子说：'一切由命运决定。'孔子依礼法而进，依道义而退，所以他说得到或得不到官位是'由命运决定'。如果他寄住在痈疽和宦官瘠环那里，这便是无视礼义和命运了。孔子在鲁国、卫国不得意，又遇到宋国的司马桓魋企图在半路上杀害他，只得更换衣着悄悄通过宋国了。这时孔子正遭危难，便寄住到司城贞子家里，做了陈侯周的臣子。我听说过，观察在朝的近臣，看他所接待住宿的是什么人；观察外来的远臣，看他所寄居处的主人。如果孔子寄住在痈疽和宦官瘠环家里，把他们当作主人，还怎么能算是孔子？”

【解读】本章主要论述关于孔子寄居处所的传言。宠臣、宦官几乎每天都能够接触到国君，有些人可能会通过他们走捷径直接面见国君。但孟子认为孔子是有原则、有操守的人，进退有标准（“进以礼，退以义”），即便有学生子路的关系在，他也不会选择这种“旁门左道”去接触国君；并且孟子也详谈了孔子在卫国寄住在颜雠由家、在陈国住在司城贞子家里的前因后果，批驳传言有理有据。大概一个政治人物的一举一动都可能含有政治意图，对于近臣，看他结交哪些人；对于远臣，则观察他选择什么人家寄居。以孔子的为人，即便其内心渴望被重用，也绝对不会通过宠臣之助来实现抱负。

9.9

万章问曰："或曰：'百里奚[1]自鬻[2]于秦养牲者，五羊之皮，食牛，以要秦穆公[3]。'信乎？"

孟子曰："否，不然。好事者为之也。百里奚，虞[4]人也。晋人以垂棘之璧与屈产之乘，假道于虞以伐虢[5]。宫之奇[6]谏，百里奚不谏。知虞公之不可谏而去，之秦，年已七十矣，曾[7]不知以食牛干秦穆公之为污也，可谓智乎？不可谏而不谏，可谓不智乎？知虞公之将亡而先去之，不可谓不智也。时举于秦，知穆公之可与有行[8]也而相之，可谓不智乎？相秦而显其君于天下，可传于后世，不贤而能之乎？自鬻以成其君，乡党自好者不为，而谓贤者为之乎？"

Wan Zhang asked Mencius, "Some say that Baili Xi sold himself to a cattle-keeper of Qin for the skins of five rams, and fed his oxen, in order to find an introduction to the duke Mu of Qin; —was this the case?"

Mencius said, "No; it was not so. This story was invented by men fond of strange things. Baili -Xi was a man of Yu. The people of Jin, by the inducement of a round piece of jade from Chuiji, and four horses of the Qu breed, borrowed a passage through Yu to attack Guo. On that occasion, Gong Zhi qi remonstrated against granting their request, and Baili Xi did not remonstrate. When he knew that the duke of Yu was not to be remonstrated with, and, leaving that State, went to Qin, he had reached the age of seventy. If by that time he did not know that it would be a mean thing to seek an introduction to the duke Mu of Qin by feeding oxen, could he be called wise? But not remonstrating where it was of no use to remonstrate, could he be said not to be wise? Knowing that the duke of Yu would be ruined, and leaving him before that event, he cannot be said not to have been wise. Being then advanced in Qin, he knew that the duke Mu was one with whom he would enjoy a field for action, and became minister to him; —could he, acting thus, be said not to be wise? Having become chief minister of Qin, he made his prince distinguished throughout the kingdom, and worthy of being handed down to future ages; — could he have done this, if he had not been a man of talents and virtue? As to selling himself in order to accomplish all the aims of his prince, even a villager who had a regard for himself would not do such a thing; and shall we say that a man of talents and virtue did it?"

【注释】［1］百里奚：曾为虞国大夫，虞亡后，奔赴秦国，辅助秦穆公建立霸业。［2］鬻（yù）：卖。［3］秦穆公：又作秦缪公，秦国国君，公元前659年—前621年在位。［4］虞：国名，在今山西平陆北。［5］垂棘：晋国地名，产美玉。屈：晋地名，产良马。乘：四匹马。虢（guó）：国名，在今河南三门峡和山西平陆一带。［6］宫之奇：虞国贤臣。晋国曾两次向虞国借路以攻打虢国，宫之奇用“唇亡齿寒”的道理劝告虞公拒绝晋的要求，虞公不听。结果晋灭虢后，接着灭掉了虞国。［7］曾：乃，竟。［8］有行：同“有为”。

【译文】万章问道：“有人说：‘百里奚把自己卖给秦国养牲口的人，用了五张羊皮的价钱，替他喂牛，以此（寻找机会）求得秦穆公任用。’这是真的吗？”

孟子说：“不，不是这样；是好事者编造的。百里奚是虞国人。当时晋国用垂棘所产的美玉和屈地所产的良马作为礼物，向虞国借路去攻打虢国。宫之奇劝虞公不要答应，百里奚不劝告。因为他知道虞公不会听从劝告，就离开虞国，到了秦国，当时已经七十岁了，如果他不知道靠给人喂牛求得秦穆公任用是不光彩的，能说他明智吗？知道虞君不会听从劝告就不去劝告，能说不明智吗？知道虞公就要亡国而先离开，不能说不明智啊。在秦国受举荐时，就知道穆公是个可以帮助而有作为的君主，因而辅佐他，能说不明智吗？做了秦国的相而使他君主的威望显赫于天下，并且可以流传到后世，不是贤者能做到这一步吗？卖掉自己去成全君主，就连乡里自爱的人也不愿干，难道说贤者肯这么干吗？”

【解读】万章所问是当时颇为流行的传说，据说百里奚在虞灭亡后以五张羊皮的价格把自己卖给秦国的牧羊人，以此寻找机会求得秦穆公的任用。孟子为百里奚做了辩解，他指出了百里奚的三个明智之处和一个贤能之举，即“不可谏而不谏”“知虞公之将亡而先去之”“知穆公之可与有行也而相之”“相秦而显其君于天下，可传于后世”。认为百里奚有准确的预见性，能看清天下大势，顺势而为而不逆势而动，是智者，也是贤者。

由此推知，他不可能做出自污其身去求取秦穆公的不智之举。这种推理究竟与事实是否一致，在此不加探究，而孟子言论中，百里奚体现出的顺势而为的做法，值得我们去借鉴思考。历史上那些在治国平天下方面有所作为的人，如诸葛亮、张居正、曾国藩等，无不是能够与世推移、与时偕行、顺势而为、善于变通的人物。

万章下

Wan Zhang 2

10.1

孟子曰："伯夷，目不视恶色，耳不听恶声。非其君不事，非其民不使。治则进，乱则退。横[1]政之所出，横民之所止，不忍居也。思与乡人处，如以朝衣朝冠坐于涂炭也。当纣之时，居北海之滨，以待天下之清也。故闻伯夷之风者，顽[2]夫廉，懦夫有立志。

"伊尹曰：'何事非君？何使非民？'治亦进，乱亦进。曰：'天之生斯民也，使先知觉后知，使先觉觉后觉。予，天民之先觉者也；予将以此道觉此民也。'思天下之民匹夫匹妇有不与被尧、舜之泽者，若己推而内之沟中，其自任以天下之重也。

"柳下惠，不羞污君，不辞小官。进不隐贤，必以其道。遗佚[3]而不怨，厄穷而不悯。与乡人处，由由然不忍去也。'尔为尔，我为我，虽袒裼裸裎[4]于我侧，尔焉能浼[5]我哉？'故闻柳下惠之风者，鄙夫宽，薄夫敦。

“孔子之去齐，接淅[6]而行；去鲁，曰：‘迟迟吾行也。’去父母国之道也。可以速而速，可以久而久，可以处而处，可以仕而仕，孔子也。”

孟子曰：“伯夷，圣之清者也；伊尹，圣之任者也；柳下惠，圣之和者也；孔子，圣之时者也。孔子之谓集大成。集大成也者，金声而玉振之也[7]。金声也者，始条理也；玉振之也者，终条理也。始条理者，智之事也；终条理者，圣之事也。智，譬则巧也；圣，譬则力也。由射于百步之外也，其至，尔力也；其中，非尔力也。”

Mencius said, “Boyi would not allow his eyes to look on a bad sight, nor his ears to listen to a bad sound. He would not serve a prince whom he did not approve, nor command a people whom he did not esteem. In a time of good government he took office, and on the occurrence of confusion he retired.

He could not bear to dwell either in a court from which a lawless government emanated, or among lawless people. He considered his being in the same place with a villager, as if he were to sit amid mud and coals with his court robes and court cap. In the time of Zhou he dwelt on the shores of the north sea, waiting the purification of the kingdom. Therefore when men now hear the character of Bo-yi, the corrupt become pure, and the weak acquire determination.

Yi Yin said, 'Whom may I not serve? My serving him makes him my sovereign. What people may I not command? My commanding them makes them my people.' In a time of good government he took office, and when confusion prevailed, he also took office. He said, 'Heaven's plan in the production of mankind is this: —that they who are first informed should instruct those who are later in being informed, and they who first apprehend principles should instruct those who are slower in doing so. I am the one of Heaven's people who has first apprehended; —I will take these principles and instruct the people in them.' He thought that among all the people of the kingdom, even the common men and women, if there were any who did not share in the enjoyment of such benefits as Yao and Shun conferred, it was as if he himself pushed them into a ditch—for he took upon himself the heavy charge of the kingdom.

Hui of Liuxia was not ashamed to serve an impure prince, nor did he think it low to be an inferior officer. When advanced to employment, he did not conceal his virtue, but made it a point to carry out his principles. When dismissed and left without office, he did not murmur. When straitened by poverty, he did not grieve. When thrown into the company of village people, he was quite at ease and could not bear to leave them. He had a saying,

'You are you, and I am I. Although you stand by my side with breast and arms bare, or with your body naked, how can you defile me?' Therefore when men now hear the character of Hui of Liuxia, the mean become generous, and the niggardly become liberal.

When Confucius was leaving Qi, he strained off with his hand the water in which his rice was being rinsed, took the rice, and went away. When he left Lu, he said, '1 will set out by and by'—it was right he should leave the country of his parents in this way. When it was proper to go away quickly, he did so; when it was proper to delay, he did so; when it was proper to keep in retirement, he did so; when it was proper to go into office, he did so: —this was Confucius."

Mencius said, "Boyi among the sages was the pure one; Yi Yin was the one most inclined to take office; Hui of Liuxia was the accommodating one; and Confucius was the timeous one. In Confucius we have what is called a complete concert. A complete concert is when the large bell proclaims the commencement of the music, and the ringing stone proclaims its close. The metal sound commences the blended harmony of all the instruments, and the winding up with the stone terminates that blended harmony. The commencing that harmony is the work of wisdom. The terminating it is the work of sageness. As a comparison for wisdom, we may liken it to skill, and as a comparison for sageness, we may liken it to strength; —as in the case of shooting at a mark a hundred paces distant. That you reach it is owing to your strength, but that you hit the mark is not owing to your strength."

【注释】［1］横（hèng）：暴。［2］顽：贪婪。［3］遗佚：不被重用。［4］袒裼（xī）裸裎（chéng）：赤身露体。［5］浼（měi）：玷污，污染。［6］淅：淘过的米。［7］金声：指镈钟发出的声音。

玉振：指玉磬（qìng）收束的余韵。古代奏乐，开始以镈钟起音，结束以玉磬收尾。

【译文】孟子说：“伯夷，眼睛不看丑恶的事物，耳朵不听丑恶的声音。不是他理想的君主他就不侍奉，不是他的百姓他就不使唤。天下大治就出来做官，天下混乱就隐居田野。施行暴政的国家，住有暴民的地方，他都不愿居住。他认为和乡下无修养的人相处，就像穿戴着朝服朝冠却坐在泥灰上一样。在纣王统治的时候，他隐居在渤海边，等待着天下清明。所以，听到过伯夷风范的人，贪得无厌的会变得廉洁，懦弱的会有定志。

“伊尹说：‘哪个君主不可以侍奉？哪个百姓不可以使唤？’所以他天下大治要做官，天下混乱也要做官。他说：‘上天生下这些民众，就是让先知道的人开导后知道的人，让先觉悟的人开导后觉悟的人。我，就是天生之民中先知先觉的人；我将要用尧舜之道开导这些人。’他想到天下的民众哪怕是匹夫匹妇没有得到尧舜之道的恩泽的，就好像是自己把他们推进沟里一样，伊尹就这样把天下的重任放在自己身上。

“柳下惠，不以侍奉坏君主为羞耻，也不因官小而不做。做官不隐藏自己的才能，一定按自己的原则办事。不被重用也不怨恨，穷困也不忧愁。与乡下人相处，他态度随和不忍离去。（他说：）‘你是你，我是我，虽然你赤身裸体在我旁边，又怎么能玷污我呢？’所以听到过柳下惠风范的人，心胸狭窄的会变得宽广起来，刻薄的会变得厚道起来。

“孔子离开齐国，捧着淘湿的米就走；离开鲁国却说：‘我要慢慢走啊。’他这是离开父母之国的方法啊。该快就快，该慢就慢，该隐居就隐居，该出仕就出仕，这就是孔子。”

孟子说：“伯夷，是圣人之中最清高的；伊尹，是圣人之中最负责任的；柳下惠，是圣人之中最随和的；孔子，是圣人之中最识时务的。孔子，可以称他为集大成者。集大成的人，就好比乐队演奏，以镈钟声开始起音，以玉磬声结束收尾。镈钟声起音是为了有条理地开始，玉磬声收尾是为了有条理地结束。有条有理地开始是智方面的事，有条有理地结束是圣方面的事。智慧，好比是技巧；圣德，好比是力量。犹如在百步以外射箭一样，能射到，是你的力量；至于射中，却不是力量（而是技巧）所能决定的。”

【解读】本章主讲孟子对先贤的评述。伯夷期待天下清明，绝不让任何污浊的东西玷污自己的清誉；伊尹以启蒙天下百姓为己任，而不论天下大治，还是大乱；柳下惠亲和大众，其亲和之风让周围的人感到舒服。而孟子认为孔子与以上三人不是并列关系，而是集诸圣之大成的人物，曰：“集大成也者，金声而玉振之也。”孔子被称为“大成至圣先师”，孔庙的主殿名“大成殿”即来源于此章。孔庙正门的“金声玉振坊”亦源于此章。

孔子集中三位圣人的优点于一身，表现为“可以速而速，可以久而久，可以处而处，可以仕而仕”，他将伯夷的清、伊尹的任及柳下惠的和，融为一体，就像一曲完美的乐章，开头由镈钟起音，结束以玉磬收尾，善始善终而条理清晰。

孔子能够在坚守其信仰和原则的前提下，既有道德修行又有政治智慧；他审时度势，与时俱进，有所坚守，却又不墨守成规。正如同射箭一样，需要力量，也需要技巧；实现理想的道路也是如此，需要“圣”，也需要“智”，孔子就是融通二者之人。这是孟子对于孔子极高的赞美，后来史学大家司马迁对孔子也有极高的赞扬，他写道：“《诗》有之：‘高山仰止，景行行止。’虽不能至，然心乡往之。余读孔氏书，想见其为人。适鲁，观仲尼庙堂车服礼器，诸生以时习礼其家，余袛回留之不能去云。天下君王至于贤人众矣，当时则荣，没则已焉。孔子布衣，传十余世，学者宗之。自天子王侯，中国言六艺者折中于夫子，可谓至圣矣！”（《史记·孔子世家》）

10.2

北宫锜[1]问曰："周室班[2]爵禄也，如之何？"

孟子曰："其详不可得闻也。诸侯恶其害己也，而皆去其籍。然而轲也，尝闻其略也。天子一位，公一位，侯一位，伯一位，子、男同一位，凡五等也。君一位，卿一位，大夫一位，上士一位，中士一位，下士一位，凡六等。天子之制，地方千里，公侯皆方百里，伯七十里，子、男五十里，凡四等。不能[3]五十里，不达于天子，附于诸侯，曰附庸。天子之卿受地视[4]侯，大夫受地视伯，元士[5]受地视子、男。大国地方百里，君十卿禄，卿禄四大夫，大夫倍上士，上士倍中士，中士倍下士，下士与庶人在官者同禄，禄足以代其耕也。次国地方七十里，君十卿禄，卿禄三大夫，大夫倍上士，上士倍中士，中士倍下士，下士与庶人在官者同禄，禄足以代其耕也。小国地方五十里，君十卿禄，卿禄二大夫，大夫倍上士，上士倍中士，中士倍下士，下士与庶人在官者同禄，禄足以代其耕也。耕者之所获，一夫百亩。百亩之粪[6]，上农夫食九人，上次食八人，中食七人，中次食六人，下食五人。庶人在官者，其禄以是为差[7]。”

Beigong Qi asked Mencius, saying, “What was the arrangement of dignities and emoluments determined by the house of Zhou?”

Mencius replied, “The particulars of that arrangement cannot be learned, for the princes, disliking them as injurious to themselves, have all made away with the records of them. Still I have learned the general outline of them. The Son of Heaven constituted one dignity; the Gong one; the Hou one; the Bai one; and the Zi and the Nan each one of equal rank: —altogether making five degrees of rank. The ruler again constituted one dignity; the chief minister one; the great officer one; the scholars of the first class one; those of the middle class one; and those of the lowest class one:—altogether making six degrees of dignity. To the Son of Heaven there was allotted a territory of a thousand *li* square. A Gong and a Hou had each a hundred *li* square. A Bai had seventy *li*, and a Zi and a Nan had each fifty *li*. The assignments altogether were of four amounts. Where the territory did not amount to fifty *li*, the chief could not have access himself to the Son of Heaven. His land was attached to some Hou-ship, and was called a Fuyong. The chief ministers of the Son of Heaven received an amount of territory equal to that of a Hou; a great officer received as much as a Bai; and a scholar of the first class as much as a Zi or a Nan. In a great state, where the territory was a hundred *li* square, the ruler had ten times as much income as his chief ministers; a chief minister four times as much as a great officer; a great officer twice as much as a scholar of the first class; a scholar of the first class twice as much as one of the middle; a scholar of the middle class twice as much as one of the lowest; the scholars of the lowest class, and such of the common people as were employed about the government offices, had for their emolument as much as was equal to what they would have made by tilling the fields. In a state of the next order, where the territory was seventy *li* square, the ruler had ten times as much revenue as his chief minister; a chief minister three times as much as a great officer; a great officer twice as much as a scholar of the first class; a scholar of the first class twice as much as one of the middle; a scholar of the middle class twice as much as one of the lowest; the scholars of the lowest class, and such of the common people as were employed about the government offices, had for their emolument as much as was equal to what they would have made by tilling the fields. In a small

state, where the territory was fifty *li* square, the ruler had ten times as much revenue as his chief minister; a chief minister had twice as much as a great officer; a great officer twice as much as a scholar of the highest class; a scholar of the highest class twice as much as one of the middle; a scholar of the middle class twice as much as one of the lowest; scholars of the lowest class, and such of the common people as were employed about the government offices, had the same emolument; —as much, namely, as was equal to what they would have made by tilling the fields. As to those who tilled the fields, each husbandman received a hundred *mu*. When those *mu* were manured, the best husbandmen of the highest class supported nine individuals, and those ranking next to them supported eight. The best husbandmen of the second class supported seven individuals, and those ranking next to them supported six; while husbandmen of the lowest class only supported five. The salaries of the common people who were employed about the government offices were regulated according to these differences."

【注释】[1]北宫锜(qí):卫国人。[2]班:颁行、规定。[3]能:及。[4]视:参照,比照。[5]元士:天子直辖区域内的上士。[6]粪:施肥。[7]差:等级,等差。

【译文】北宫锜问道:“周朝颁布的官爵和俸禄的等级,是怎样的?”

孟子说:“详细情况已经不能知道了。诸侯们都讨厌它妨害自己的利益,便把那些典籍都毁掉了。不过我曾经听说过它的大致情况。天子一级,公爵一级,侯爵一级,伯爵一级,子爵、男爵同一级,共五个等级。(诸侯国里)国君一级,卿一级,大夫一级,上士一级,中士一级,下士一级,共六个等级。天子的土地规模,方圆千里,公爵、侯爵都是方圆百里，伯爵是方圆七十里，子爵、男爵是方圆五十里，共四等。不足方圆五十里的国家，不直属于天子，而是附属于诸侯，叫作附庸。天子的卿受封土地同侯爵相等，大夫受封的土地同伯爵相等，元士受封的土地同子爵、男爵相等。大的诸侯国土地有方圆百里，国君的俸禄是卿的十倍，卿的俸禄是大夫的四倍，大夫是上士的两倍，上士是中士的两倍，中士是下士的两倍，下士的俸禄同在官府当差的百姓相同，数量足以代替他种田的收入。中等的诸侯国土地有方圆七十里，国君的俸禄是卿的十倍，卿的俸禄是大夫的三倍，大夫是上士的两倍，上士是中士的两倍，中士是下士的两倍，下士同在官府当差的同等俸禄，俸禄足以代替他种田的收入。小的诸侯国土地有方圆五十里，国君的俸禄是卿的十倍，卿的俸禄是大夫的两倍，大夫是上士的两倍，上士是中士的两倍，中士是下士的两倍，下士同在官府当差的百姓俸禄相等，俸禄足以代替他种田的收入。种田人的收入，一个农夫受田一百亩。一百亩地施肥耕种，上等的农夫可以养活九人，次于上等的可以养活八人，中等的农夫可以养活七人，次于中等的可以养活六人，下等的农夫可以养活五人。在官府当差的百姓，他的俸禄是按这种区别来分等级。”

【解读】分封制为周朝数百年的统治提供了制度保障，后来随着铁器时代的到来，生产力得到极大解放，分封制已不再适应当时的社会需求。各大诸侯国有了新的目的和追求，不再满足于分封制带来的利益，于是分封制开始逐步瓦解。春秋末年到战国时期，大国兼并小国，同姓国也相互攻伐，各诸侯国为了摆脱周王室的制度枷锁，把那些记录周代制度的典籍都销毁了。孟子对周代制度的追忆为后人研究周代官爵和俸禄的等级在一定程度上提供了史料（但真实性仍需要考证，在此不做赘述）。

通过孟子的回忆，我们可以看到周朝官爵和俸禄等级的严密性，而如此理想化的制度很有可能难以现实，最终陷入僵化。不论什么样的国家，不论任何时代，都必须有一定的社会规范。这个规范必须立足于经济基础之上，并根据现实情况不断调整，如此国家方可稳固。这也启发我们，任何制度都有其历史局限性，所以要不断根据客观现实做出改革创新，改革只有进行时，没有完成时。

10.3

万章问曰："敢问友。"

孟子曰："不挟[1]长，不挟贵，不挟兄弟而友。友也者，友其德也，不可以有挟也。孟献子[2]，百乘之家也，有友五人焉：乐正裘、牧仲，其三人，则予忘之矣。献子之与此五人者友也，无献子之家者也。此五人者，亦有献子之家，则不与之友矣。非惟百乘之家为然也，虽小国之君亦有之。费[3]惠公曰：'吾于子思，则师之矣；吾于颜般，则友之矣；王顺、长息则事我者也。'非惟小国之君为然也，虽大国之君亦有之。晋平公之于亥唐[4]也，入云则入，坐云则坐，食云则食。虽蔬食[5]菜羹，未尝不饱，盖不敢不饱也，然终于此而已矣。弗与共天位也，弗与治天职也，弗与食天禄也，士之尊贤者也，非王公之尊贤也。舜尚[6]见帝，帝馆甥[7]于贰室[8]，亦飨舜，迭为宾主，是天子而友匹夫也。用下敬上，谓之贵贵；

用上敬下，谓之尊贤。贵贵、尊贤，其义一也。”

Wan Zhang asked Mencius, saying, “I venture to ask the principles of friendship.”

Mencius replied, “Friendship should be maintained without any presumption on the ground of one's superior age, or station, or the circumstances of his relatives. Friendship with a man is friendship with his virtue, and does not admit of assumptions of superiority. There was Meng Xian, chief of a family of a hundred chariots. He had five friends, namely, Yuezheng Qiu, Mu Zhong, and three others whose names I have forgotten. With those five men Xian maintained a friendship, because they thought nothing about his family. If they had thought about his family, he would not have maintained his friendship with them. Not only has the chief of a family of a hundred chariots acted thus. The same thing was exemplified by the sovereign of a small state. The duke Hui of Bi said, 'I treat Zisi as my teacher, and Yan Ban as my friend. As to Wang Shun and Chang Xi, they serve me.' Not only has the sovereign of a small state acted thus. The same thing has been exemplified by the sovereign of a large state. There was the duke Ping of Jin with Hai Tang: —when Tang told him to come into his house, he came; when he told him to be seated, he sat; when he told him to eat, he ate. There might only be coarse rice and soup of vegetables, but he always ate his fill, not daring to do otherwise. Here, however, he stopped, and went no farther. He did not call him to share any of Heaven's places, or to govern any of Heaven's offices, or to partake of any of Heaven's emoluments. His conduct was but a scholar's honouring virtue and talents, not the honouring them proper to a king or a duke. Shun went up to court and saw the sovereign, who lodged him as his son-in-law in the second palace. The sovereign also enjoyed there Shun's hospitality. Alternately he was host and guest. Here was the sovereign maintaining friendship with a private man. Respect shown by inferiors to superiors is called giving to the noble the observance due to rank. Respect shown by superiors to inferiors is called giving honour to talents and virtue. The rightness in each case is the same."

【注释】[1]挟：倚仗。[2]孟献子：鲁国大夫仲孙蔑。[3]费：春秋时小国。[4]亥唐：晋国人。晋平公时，朝中多贤臣，但亥唐不愿为官，隐居穷巷，平公闻其贤，对他非常敬重。[5]蔬食：粗糙的饮食。蔬同"疏"。[6]尚：同"上"。[7]甥：古时称妻子的父亲叫外舅，所以女婿也被称为"甥"，舜是尧帝的女婿。[8]贰室：副宫，即招待宫邸。

【译文】万章问道："请问交友的原则。"

孟子说："不倚仗年长，不倚仗位高，

不倚仗兄弟（的成就）去交友。交友，交往的是品德，不可以有什么倚仗。孟献子，是一位拥有百辆车马的大夫，他有五位友人：乐正裘、牧仲，其余三位，我忘记了。献子与这五人相交，并没有倚仗自己的身份。这五个人如果考虑献子的身份，那也就不与献子交友了。不仅具有百辆车马的大夫如此，即便小国的国君也有这样的。费惠公说：‘我对于子思，把他尊为老师；我对于颜般，和他交友；王顺和长息，则是侍奉我的人。’不仅小国的国君如此，即便大国的国君也有这样的。晋平公对待亥唐，亥唐叫他进去就进去，叫他坐就坐，叫他吃就吃。即使是粗糙简陋的食物，未曾不吃饱，大概不敢不吃饱。不过，晋平公也就是做到这一步而已。不同他一起共享君主之位，不同他一起治理政事，不同他一起享受俸禄，这只是一般士人尊敬贤者的态度，而不是王公贵族对贤者的态度。舜去拜见尧帝，尧让舜住在副宫中，又设宴

款待舜，（舜设宴回敬尧帝）二人互为宾主，这是天子与普通百姓交友的范例。地位低下的人尊敬地位高贵的人，这叫尊敬贵人；地位高贵的人尊敬地位低下的人，这叫尊敬贤人。尊敬贵人和尊敬贤人，道理都是一样的。”

【解读】本章中万章向孟子请教交友之道，孟子就向万章阐述了交友的原则，即“不挟长，不挟贵，不挟兄弟而友”。交友应该“友其德”，不可以掺杂金钱、地位等利害关系。古人非常重视这一点，并多有论述，如“以财交者，财尽而交绝；以色交者，华落而爱渝”（《战国策·楚策一》），“以权利合者，权利尽而交疏”（《史记·郑世家》）。不仅一般的百姓如此，居官从政者更应当如此。孟子强调“贵贵”是贵贵人之德，“尊贤”是尊贤人之德，不论社会地位高低，重在有德。古人云：“与善人居，如入芝兰之室，久而不闻其香，即与之化矣。与不善人居，如入鲍鱼之肆，久而不闻其臭，亦与之化矣。丹之所藏者赤，漆之所藏者黑，是以君子必慎其所与处者焉。”（《孔子家语·六本》）所以，“德”无疑是择友时最重要的衡量标准。交友不慎可能导致祸患，一些别有用心的人与其说是“交友”，不如说是“交易”。“友谊的小船”在背离初心的航道上渐行渐远，说翻就翻。《庄子·山木》中云：“君子之交淡若水，小人之交甘若醴；君子淡以亲，小人甘以绝。彼无故以合者，则无故以离。”纯粹而澄澈的友谊才是我们应当向往和追求的。

10.4

万章问曰："敢问交际[1]何心也？"

孟子曰："恭也。"

曰："却[2]之却之为不恭，何哉？"

曰："尊者赐之，曰'其所取之者，义乎，不义乎'，而后受之，以是为不恭，故弗却也。"

曰："请无以辞却之，以心却之，曰'其取诸民之不义也'，而以他辞无受，不可乎？"

曰："其交也以道，其接也以礼，斯孔子受之矣。"

万章曰："今有御[3]人于国门之外者，其交也以道，其馈也以礼，斯可受御与？"

曰："不可。《康诰》[4]曰：'杀越[5]人于货，闵[6]不畏死，凡民罔不譈[7]。'是不待教而诛者也。殷受夏，周受殷，所不辞也；于今为烈[8]，如之何其受之？"

曰："今之诸侯取之于民也，犹御也。苟善其礼际矣，斯君子受之，敢问何说也？"

曰："子以为有王者作，将比[9]今之诸侯而诛之乎？其教之不改而后诛之乎？夫谓非其有而取之者盗也，充类至义[10]之尽也。孔子之仕于鲁也，鲁人猎较[11]，孔子亦猎较。猎较犹可，而况受其赐乎？"

曰："然则孔子之仕也，非事道[12]与？"

曰："事道也。"

"事道奚猎较也？"

曰："孔子先簿正祭器，不以四方之食供簿正。"

曰："奚不去也？"

曰："为之兆[13]也。兆足以行矣，而不行，而后去，是以未尝有所终三年淹也。孔子有见行可之仕，有际可[14]之仕，有公养[15]之仕。于季桓子[16]，见行可之仕也；于卫灵公，际可之仕也；于卫孝公，公养之仕也。"

Wan Zhang asked Mencius, saying, "I venture to ask what feeling of the mind is expressed in the presents of friendship?"

Mencius replied, "The feeling of respect."

"How is it," pursued Zhang, "that the declining a present is accounted disrespectful?"

The answer was, "When one of honourable rank presents a gift, to say in the mind, 'Was the way in which he got this righteous or not? I must know this before I can receive it'—this is deemed disrespectful, and therefore presents are not declined."

Wan Zhang asked again, "When one does not take on him in so many express words to refuse the gift, but having declined it in his heart, saying, 'It was taken by him unrighteously from the people,' and then assigns some other reason for not receiving it;—is not this a proper course?"

Mencius said, "When the donor offers it on a ground of reason, and his manner of doing so is according to propriety,—in such a case Confucius would have received it."

Wan Zhang said, "Here now is one who stops and robs people outside the gates of the city. He offers his gift on a ground of reason, and does so in a manner according to propriety; —would the reception of it so acquired by robbery be proper?"

Mencius replied, "It would not be proper. In *the Announcement to Kang* it is said, 'When men kill others, and roll over their bodies to take their property, being reckless and fearless of death, among all the people there are none but detest them.'— Thus, such characters are to be put to death, without waiting to give them warning. Yin received this rule from Xia and Zhou received it from Yin. It cannot be questioned, and to the present day is clearly acknowledged. How can the gift of a robber be received?"

Wan Zhang said, "The princes of the present day take from their people just as a robber despoils his victim. Yet if they put a good face of propriety on their gifts, then the superior man receives them. I venture to ask how you explain this."

Mencius answered, "Do you think that, if there should arise a truly royal sovereign, he would collect the princes of the present day, and put them all to death? Or would he admonish them, and then, on their not changing their ways, put them to death? Indeed, to call every one who takes what does not properly belong to him a robber, is pushing a point of resemblance to the utmost, and insisting on the most refined idea of righteousness. When Confucius was in office in Lu, the people struggled together for the game taken in hunting, and he also did the same. If that struggling for the captured game was proper, how much more may the gifts of the princes be received!"

Wan Zhang urged, "Then are we to suppose that when Confucius held office, it was not with the view to carry his doctrines into practice?"

"It was with that view," Mencius replied,

And Wan Zhang rejoined, "If the practice of his doctrines was his business, what had he to do with that struggling for the captured game?"

Mencius said, "Confucius first rectified his vessels of sacrifice according to the registers, and did not fill them so rectified with food gathered from every quarter."

Wan Zhang said, "But why did he not go away?"

Mencius said, "He wished to make a trial of carrying his doctrines into practice. When that trial was sufficient to show that they could be practised and they were still not practised, then he went away, and thus it was that he never completed in any state a residence of three years. Confucius took office when he saw that the practice of his doctrines was likely; he took office when his reception was proper; he took office when he was supported by the state. In the case of his relation to Ji Huan, he took office, seeing that the practice of his doctrines was likely. With the duke Ling of Wei he took office, because his reception was proper. With the duke Xiao of Wei he took office, because he was maintained by the state."

【注释】［1］交际：交往。际：接。［2］却：推辞不接受。［3］御：拦截。［4］《康诰》：《尚书》篇名。［5］越：抢劫。［6］闵：强横。［7］譈（duì）：怨，怨恨。［8］于今为烈：从"殷受夏"到"于今为烈"十四字，朱熹认为是衍文，可略而不论。［9］比：连。［10］充类至义：充其类，极其义，指把标准提升到最高点。［11］猎较（jué）：古代打猎时，相互炫耀所猎获的猎物，并用于祭祀。［12］事道：以行道为志向。［13］兆：始，开端。［14］际可：以礼交接。［15］公养：国君以养贤之礼奉养贤者。［16］季桓子：名斯，春秋时期鲁国大夫。

【译文】万章问道："请问，同别人交往要抱什么样的心态？"

孟子说："恭敬的心态。"

（万章）问："一再拒绝就是不恭敬，为什么呢？"

（孟子）说："有地位的人赐给礼物，自己暗自说'他得来这些东西是符合义的呢，还是不符合义的呢'，然后才接受，（人们）认为这是不恭敬的，所以不要拒绝。"

（万章）说："如果不用言语拒绝，而在心里拒绝，暗自说'他从百姓那里取来的这些东西是不义的'，然后用别的理由拒绝接受，不行吗？"

（孟子）说："如果相互交往符合道，接待也符合礼，即便是孔子也会接受的。"

万章说："如果有个在城门外拦路抢劫的人，他以符合道的方式与我们交往，以符合礼的方式接待我们，这样也可以接受他抢来的东西吗？"

（孟子）说："不行。《康诰》上说：'杀人抢劫，强横不怕死的人，人们没有不痛恨的。'这种人是不必等候教育就可以处死的。（这种规定）殷朝从夏朝继承来，周朝从殷朝继承来，没有拒绝继承的；现在对此类坏人的惩罚更加严厉，怎么还能接受他的东西呢？"

（万章）说："现在的诸侯从百姓那里掠取财物，就像拦路抢劫一样。如果他们按照礼节交往，这样君子就可以接受他们的礼物，请问这又怎么说呢？"

（孟子）说："你认为如果有圣王出现，他将会把现在的诸侯统统杀掉呢？还是把经过教育仍不悔改的诸侯杀掉呢？认为不是他该有的东西他拿了，这就是抢劫，这是把'抢劫'的含义范围扩大到极致了。孔子在鲁国做官时，鲁国人有打猎时争夺猎物的习俗，孔子也去争夺了。争夺猎物尚且可以，何况接受别人赠给的礼物呢？"

（万章）说："那么孔子做官，不是为

了行道吗？”

（孟子）说：“是为了行道。”

（万章）说：“行道何必去争夺猎物呢？”

（孟子）说：“孔子先用文书规定该用的祭器，（规定）不用四方珍奇的猎物充作祭品。”

（万章）说：“孔子为什么不辞官离开呢？”

（孟子）说：“为了试行（自己的主张）。试行的结果足以行得通，君主却不推行，这才离开那里，所以孔子不曾有在某个国家做官满三年的。孔子有时因为看到有行道的可能而去做官，有时因为君主对他以礼相待而去做官，有时因为君主能供养贤士而去做官。对于季桓子，是有行道的可能而去做官；对于卫灵公，是他能以礼相待而去做官；对于卫孝公，是他能供养贤士而去做官。”

【解读】本章中孟子讲解在交友过程中产生的

辞受问题，并由此而涉及认识诸侯和入仕等问题。孟子首先指出要以恭敬的心态接受别人的馈赠，如果能做到“其交也以道，其接也以礼”便很好了；同时，孟子也指出对于杀人越货取得的财富要坚决拒绝。《论语》有云：“富与贵是人之所欲也，不以其道得之，不处也。”（《论语·里仁》）明代贤臣黄绾恪守儒家关于富贵、贫贱的判断标准，主张以“道、义”作为“辞受、取与”与“治生、作务”的行为准则。

面对弟子万章接连的尖锐问题，孟子还阐述了诸侯与强盗的区别，孟子提醒万章不能把强盗的定义无限扩大，而且对于诸侯无义的剥削行为应该先教之而后才可惩戒。孟子的见解无疑是务实的，他虽然是完美的理想主义者，但也有现实的一面。对分析孔子做官的缘由，孟子将其概括为“有见行可之仕”“有际可之仕”“有公养之仕”，对于这些情况，孔子均是因有可能试行自己的主张才选择的。

10.5

孟子曰："仕非为贫也，而有时乎为贫；娶妻非为养也，而有时乎为养。为贫者，辞尊居卑，辞富居贫。辞尊居卑，辞富居贫，恶乎宜乎？抱关击柝[1]。孔子尝为委吏[2]矣，曰：'会计当而已矣。'尝为乘田[3]矣，曰：'牛羊茁壮，长而已矣。'位卑而言高，罪也；立乎人之本朝，而道不行，耻也。"

Mencius said, "Office is not sought on account of poverty, yet there are times when one seeks office on that account. Marriage is not entered into for the sake of being attended to by the wife, yet there are times when one marries on that account. He who takes office on account of his poverty must decline an honourable situation and occupy a low one; he must decline riches and prefer to be poor. What office will be in harmony with this declining an honourable situation and occupying a low one, this declining riches and preferring to be poor? Such an one as that of guarding the gates, or beating the watchman's stick. Confucius was once keeper of stores, and he then said, 'My calculations must be all right. That is all I have to care about.' He was once in charge of the public fields, and he then said, 'The oxen and sheep must be fat and strong, and superior. That is all I have to care about.' When one is in a low situation, to speak of high matters is a crime. When a scholar stands in a prince's court, and his principles are not carried into practice, it is a shame to him."

【注释】［1］抱关：守门人。击柝（tuò）：巡夜打更人。柝：梆子。［2］委吏：管理仓库的小官。［3］乘田：管理牲畜的小官。

【译文】孟子说："做官不是因为贫穷，但有

孔子职司乘田　于志学 绘

时却是因为贫穷；娶妻不是为了奉养父母，但有时却是为了奉养父母。因为贫穷而做官，就该不做高官而做小官，不要高薪安于薄禄。不做高官做小官，不要高薪安于薄禄，干哪样事情最适宜呢？守门打更就行了。孔子曾经做过管仓库的小吏，说道：‘账目无误即可。’又曾经做过管理牲畜的小吏，说道：‘牛羊长得肥壮即可。’地位低下而议论朝政，是罪过；在君主的朝廷上做官，而政治主张不能推行，是耻辱。”

【解读】读书人为什么做官？主要是为了实现治国平天下的理想，但有时为生计所迫也会出仕做官；而如果仅仅是解决生计问题，那就做个“抱关击柝”“委吏”“乘田”之类的小官，其标准并不高，做起来也不难，养家糊口即可。孟子强调的是“立乎人之本朝，而道不行，耻也”。居高位做大官就要为了实现自己的政治抱负，“立乎人之本朝”就不能只管俸禄薪水了，应该以社稷苍生为己任，发表自己的政见，尽到自己的一份责任，故政治主张不能推行，这就是耻辱了。但孟子思想也有其不当之处，他所讲“位卑而言高，罪也”，继承了孔子“不在其位，不谋其政”的观点，是不足取的。陆放翁讲的“位卑未敢忘忧国”，顾炎武所言“保天下者，匹夫之贱与有责焉耳矣”，则更胜一筹。时代发展到今天，无论做大官、小官，凡是为政者都应当恪守职责，做好本职工作，不做不作为的“太平官”、推诿扯皮的“滑头官”和贪图享受的“逍遥官”。

10.6

万章曰："士之不托诸侯，何也？"

孟子曰："不敢也。诸侯失国，而后托于诸侯，礼也；士之托于诸侯，非礼也。"

万章曰："君馈之粟，则受之乎？"

曰："受之。"

"受之何义也？"

曰："君之于氓[1]也，固周[2]之。"

曰："周之则受，赐之则不受，何也？"

曰："不敢也。"

曰："敢问其不敢何也？"

曰："抱关击柝者，皆有常职以食于上。无常职而赐于上者，以为不恭也。"

曰："君馈之，则受之，不识可常继乎？"

曰："缪公[3]之于子思也，亟[4]问，亟馈鼎肉[5]。子思不悦。于卒也，摽[6]使者出诸大门之外，北面稽首再拜[7]而不受，曰：'今而后知君之犬马畜伋。'盖自是台[8]

无馈也。悦贤不能举，又不能养也，可谓悦贤乎？”

曰：“敢问国君欲养君子，如何斯可谓养矣？”

曰：“以君命将之，再拜稽首而受。其后廪人[9]继粟，庖人[10]继肉，不以君命将之。子思以为鼎肉使己仆仆[11]尔亟拜也，非养君子之道也。尧之于舜也，使其子九男事之，二女女焉，百官牛羊仓廪备，以养舜于畎亩之中，后举而加[12]诸上位。故曰，王公之尊贤者也。”

Wan Zhang said, “What is the reason that a scholar does not accept a stated support from a prince?”

Mencius replied, “He does not presume to do so. When a prince loses his state, and then accepts a stated support from another prince, this is in accordance with propriety. But for a scholar to accept such support from any of the princes is not in accordance with propriety."

Wan Zhang said, "If the prince sends him a present of grain, for instance, does he accept it?"

"He accepts it," answered Mencius.

"On what principle of righteousness does he accept it?"

"Why—the prince ought to assist the people in their necessities."

Wan Zhang pursued, "Why is it that the scholar will thus accept the prince's help, but will not accept his pay?"

The answer was, "He does not presume to do so."

Wan Zhang said, "I venture to ask why he does not presume to do so."

Mencius said, "Even the keepers of the gates, with their watchmen's sticks, have their regular offices for which they can take their support from the prince. He who without a regular office should receive the pay of the prince must be deemed disrespectful."

Wan Zhang asked, "If the prince sends a scholar a present, he accepts it; —I do not know whether this present may be constantly repeated."

Mencius answered, "There was the conduct of the duke Mu to Zisi. He made frequent inquiries after Zisi's health, and sent him frequent presents of cooked meat. Zisi was displeased; and at length, having motioned to the messenger to go outside the great door, he bowed his head to the ground with his face to the north, did obeisance twice, and declined the gift, saying, 'From this time forth I shall know that the prince supports me as a dog or a horse.' And so from that time a servant was no more sent with the presents. When a prince professes to be pleased with a man of talents and virtue, and can neither promote him to office, nor support him in the proper way, can he be said to be pleased with him?"

Wan Zhang said, "I venture to ask how the sovereign of a state, when he wishes to support a superior man, must proceed, that he may be said to do so in the proper way?"

Mencius answered, "At first, the present must be offered with the prince's commission, and the scholar, making obeisance twice with his head bowed to the ground, will receive it. But after this the storekeeper will continue to send grain, and the master of the kitchen to send meat, presenting it as if without the prince's express commission. Zisi considered that the meat from the prince's caldron, giving him the annoyance of constantly doing obeisance, was not the way to support a superior man. There was Yao's conduct to Shun: —He caused his nine sons to serve him, and gave him his two daughters in marriage; he caused the various officers, oxen and sheep, storehouses and granaries, all to be prepared to support Shun amid the channelled fields, and then he raised him to the most exalted situation. From this we have the expression,—The honouring of virtue and talents proper to a king or a duke.' "

【注释】［1］氓（méng）：从他国来本国侨居的百姓。［2］周：周济。［3］缪公：鲁缪公。［4］亟（qì）：屡次。［5］鼎肉：熟肉。［6］摽（biāo）：挥之使离去。［7］稽（qǐ）首再拜：古代跪坐，相见行礼时，双手交叠，拜头至地谓之稽首；既跪而拱手，而头俯至于手，与心平，谓之拜。再拜：拜两次。"稽首再拜"谓之凶拜，表示不接受礼物。［8］台：贱官，负责使令工作。［9］廪人：管理仓库的小官。［10］庖人：厨师。［11］仆仆：劳顿不已。［12］加：放在上面。

【译文】万章问道："士人不能依附诸侯，为什么呢？"

孟子说："因为不敢。诸侯丢了国家后，寄居到别国诸侯那里生活，是合乎礼的；但士人依附诸侯，是不合乎礼的。"

万章问："如果是国君送给他谷米，那么能接受吗？"

（孟子）说："能接受。"

（万章问：）"能接受是根据什么道理？"

（孟子）说："国君对于别国迁居来的人，本来就该周济。"

（万章）说："周济他，就接受；赏赐他，就不接受，这又是什么道理？"

（孟子）说："因为不敢。"

（万章）问："请问，不敢接受是什么原因？"

（孟子）说："守门打更的人都有一定的职务，因此靠上面供养，没有一定的职务而接受上面的赏赐，被认为是不恭敬的。"

（万章）问："国君馈赠的就接受，不知是否可以经常这么做？"

（孟子）说：“鲁缪公对于子思，多次问候，多次赠送肉食。子思很不高兴。最后，子思把缪公派来的人赶出大门外，面朝北跪下磕头，然后拱手拜了两拜，拒绝接受礼物，说：‘如今才知道君王是把我当犬马一样畜养的。’打这以后就不让台吏给子思送东西了。喜爱贤士，却不提拔任用他，又不能按恰当的方式供养他，能说是喜爱贤士吗？”

（万章）说：“请问国君想要供养君子，怎样做才算是适宜的供养呢？”

（孟子）说：“（开始时）以国君名义送去，他便拱手拜两拜，跪下磕头接受。以后就让粮仓的小吏不断去送粮，厨师不断去送肉，而不必再以国君名义去送。子思认为为了那点儿肉使得自己一次接一次地跪拜行礼，这不是供养君子的恰当做法。尧对于舜，派自己的九个儿子去侍奉他，把两个女儿嫁给他，百官、牛羊、粮食均已齐备，在田野中供养他，然后提拔他，让他居于很高的职位。

所以说，这是天子诸侯尊敬贤人的正确方法。”

【解读】战国之时，战争频发，兼并激烈，各诸侯国为了提高国力，四处网罗人才为己所用，形成了养士之风。这个士人群体，包括学士、方士、策士或术士、食客等。本章中孟子以鲁缪公对于子思和尧对于舜两个事例，一反一正，具体谈论国君应该如何来养士。

士应该有尊严地活着，国君周济士要维护士的尊严，不能将其当作牛马般地畜养。《南史·陶弘景传》中提到，南朝时期“山中宰相”陶弘景辞官归隐，梁武帝萧衍亲手写诏聘请陶弘景入朝为官，并赐他鹿皮巾，后屡加礼聘，陶弘景终是不应，并画了一幅双牛图给武帝。图上一牛散放水草之间，一牛著金络头，有人执绳以杖驱。武帝见图笑曰：“此人无所求，欲效曳尾龟，岂有可致之理耶！”于是不再提聘官之事，然而每遇大事，无不前往咨询。

武帝与陶弘景之间，书信不断，有时

候一月好几封书信。孟子认为维护士的尊严是养士的最低要求，而重用以使其有发挥之平台，则是养士的最好办法。孔子在卫国时，卫灵公一方面对他很客气，给他“致粟六万”的优待，一方面却不信任重用他。孔子走后，卫灵公又想起孔子的好，再把他接回卫国。但这一次，卫灵公对孔子连基本的礼貌都没有了，“见蜚雁，仰视之，色不在孔子”。卫灵公只有一个爱才惜才的虚名却没有重用孔子，孔子对没得到卫灵公的重用也深感惋惜。

毋庸置疑，不论社会发展到什么程度，人才都是社会发展的重要生产力。人才是一个国家、民族兴旺发达的有力支撑，所以国家要培养人才、尊重人才，促使人尽其才。

10.7

万章曰："敢问不见诸侯，何义也？"

孟子曰："在国曰市井之臣，在野曰草莽之臣，皆谓庶人。庶人不传质[1]为臣，不敢见于诸侯，礼也。"

万章曰："庶人，召之役，则往役；君欲见之，召之，则不往见之，何也？"

曰："往役，义也；往见，不义也。且君之欲见之也，何为也哉？"

曰："为其多闻也，为其贤也。"

曰："为其多闻也，则天子不召师，而况诸侯乎？为其贤也，则吾未闻欲见贤而召之也。缪公亟见于子思，曰：'古千乘之国以友士，何如？'子思不悦，曰：'古之人有言：曰事之云乎，岂曰友之云乎？'子思之不悦也，岂不曰：'以位，则子，君也；我，臣也。何敢与君友也？以德，则子事我者也，奚可以与我友？'千乘之君求与之友而不可得也，而况可召与？齐景公田，招虞人[2]以旌，不至，将杀之。志士不忘在沟壑，勇士不忘丧其元[3]。孔子奚取焉？取非其招不往也。”

曰：“敢问招虞人何以？”

曰：“以皮冠，庶人以旃，士以旂，大夫以旌[4]。以大夫之招招虞人，虞人死不敢往；以士之招招庶人，庶人岂敢往哉？况乎以不贤人之招招贤人乎？欲见贤人而不以其道，犹欲其入而闭之门也。夫义，路也；礼，门也。惟君子能由是路，出入是门也。《诗》云：‘周道如底，其直如矢；君子所履，小人所视。’”

万章曰：“孔子，君命召，不俟驾而行。然则孔子非与？”

曰：“孔子当仕有官职，而以其官召之也。”

Wan Zhang said, “I venture to ask what principle of righteousness is involved in a scholar's not going to see the princes?”

Mencius replied, “A scholar residing in the city

is called 'a minister of the marketplace and well,' and one residing in the country is called 'a minister of the grass and plants.' In both cases he is a common man, and it is the rule of propriety that common men, who have not presented the introductory present and become ministers, should not presume to have interviews with the prince."

Wan Zhang said, "If a common man is called to perform any service, he goes and performs it; how is it that a scholar, when the prince, wishing to see him, calls him to his presence, refuses to go?"

Mencius replied, "It is right to go and perform the service; it would not be right to go and see the prince. And," added Mencius, "on what account is it that the prince wishes to see the scholar?"

Wan Zhang said, "Because of his extensive information, or because of his talents and virtue," was the reply.

Mencius replied, "If because of his extensive

information," said Mencius, "such a person is a teacher, and the sovereign would not call him; — how much less may any of the princes do so? If because of his talents and virtue, then I have not heard of any one wishing to see a person with those qualities, and calling him to his presence. During the frequent interviews of the duke Mu with Zisi, he one day said to him, 'Anciently, princes of a thousand chariots have yet been on terms of friendship with scholars; —what do you think of such an intercourse?' Zisi was displeased, and said, 'The ancients have said, The scholar should be served: how should they have merely said that he should be made a friend of?' When Zisi was thus displeased, did he not say within himself, With regard to our stations, you are sovereign, and I am subject. How can I presume to be on terms of friendship with my sovereign! With regard to our virtue, you ought to make me your master. How can you be on terms of friendship with me? Thus, when a ruler of a thousand chariots sought to be on terms of friendship with a scholar, he could not obtain his wish—how much less could he call him to his presence! The duke Jing of Qi, once, when he was hunting, called his forester to him by a flag. The forester would not come, and the duke was going to kill him. With reference to this incident, Confucius said, The determined officer never forgets that his end may be in a ditch or a stream; the brave officer never forgets that he may lose his head.' What was it in the forester that Confucius thus approved? He approved his not going to the duke, when summoned by the article which was not appropriate to him."

Wan Zhang said, "May I ask with what a forester should be summoned?"

Mencius replied, "With a skin cap. A common man should be summoned with a plain banner; a scholar who has taken office, with one having dragons embroidered on it; and a great officer, with one having feathers suspended from the top of the staff. When the forester was summoned with the article appropriate to the summoning of a great officer, he would have died rather than presume to go. If a common man were summoned with the article appropriate to the summoning of a scholar, how could he presume to go? How much more may we expect this refusal to go, when a man of talents and virtue is summoned in a way which is inappropriate to his character! When a prince wishes to see a man of talents and virtue, and does not take the proper course to get his wish, it is as if he wished him to enter his palace, and shut the door against him. Now, righteousness is the way, and propriety is the door, but it is only the superior man who can follow this way, and go out and in by this door. It is said in the *Book of Poetry*, 'The way to Zhou is level like a whetstone, and straight as an arrow. The officers tread it, and the lower people see it.' "

Wan Zhang said, "When Confucius received the prince's message calling him, he went without waiting for his carriage. Doing so, did Confucius do wrong?"

Mencius replied, "Confucius was in office, and had to observe its appropriate duties. And moreover, he was summoned on the business of his office."

【注释】［1］传质：求见君主的人将献给君主的见面礼品交给通报的人，由他传送进去，称为“传质”。［2］虞人：管理猎场的小吏。［3］元：头颅。［4］皮冠：打猎时所戴的帽子。旃（zhān）：古代一种没有装饰，用全幅红绸做的曲柄旗。旂（qí）：带有铃铛的旗子，上有二龙相交的图案。旌：用羽毛装饰杆头的旗子。

【译文】万章说："请问（士人）不去谒见诸侯，有什么道理吗？"

孟子说："（不在职的士人）住在都城的叫市井之臣，住在农村的叫草莽之臣，都算是百姓。百姓不向诸侯传送见面礼而成为臣属，就不敢谒见诸侯，这是礼的规定。"

万章说："百姓，召他服役，就去服役；国君要见他，召他去，却不去见，为什么呢？"

（孟子）说："去服役，是应该的义务；（不是臣属而）去见国君，是不应该的。再说国君要召见他，是因为什么呢？"

（万章）说："因为他见识广博，因为他贤能。"

（孟子）说："因为他见识广博，（便以他为师）天子尚且不能随便召见老师，何况诸侯呢？因为他贤能，那我还从来没听说过要见贤人竟要用召唤的方式。鲁缪公多次去见子思，对他说：'古代有千辆兵车的国君去跟士人交朋友，怎么样？'子思很不高兴，说：‘古人有句话：说的是侍奉他（把他当老师），哪能声称同他是朋友呢？’子思之所以不高兴，难道不是说：‘论地位，你是国君，我是臣，我怎么敢同国君交朋友呢？论道德，那么你该把我当老师侍奉，怎么可以说同我交朋友？’有千辆兵车的国君要求同他交朋友尚且办不到，更何况召他来见呢？从前齐景公打猎，用旌旗召唤管理园囿的小吏，小吏不来，齐景公要杀他。（孔子称赞他说）志士不怕弃尸山沟，勇士不怕丧失头颅。孔子赞扬他哪一点呢？赞扬他不接受不合礼制的召唤。”

（万章）说：“请问，召唤管理园囿的小吏该用什么？”

（孟子）说：“用皮帽子。召唤百姓用大红绸的曲柄旗，召唤士人用有铃铛的旗，召唤大夫用饰有羽毛的旌旗。用召唤大夫的旌旗去召管理园囿的小吏，小吏是死也不敢去的；用召唤士人的旗子去召百姓，百姓难道敢去吗？更何况用不尊重人的召唤方式去召唤贤人呢？想见贤人而不按合适的方式，那就像要人进来却又把他关在门外。义，好比是路；礼，好比是门。只有君子能沿着这条路走，从这个门进出。《诗经》上说：‘大路平得像磨刀石，直得像箭；君子所走的道路，一般人也会效法。’”

万章说：“孔子，国君召见他，他不等车马驾好就动身。那么，孔子是错了吗？”

（孟子）说：“（那时）孔子正在做官，有官职，而（国君）是按他的官职召见他的。”

【解读】本章通过对庶人与诸侯、贤士与君主之间觐见、召见问题的辨析，说明了相关礼仪规范，揭示了贤士与国君的相处之道。按照礼节，庶人是不能直接面见诸侯的，除非被传质为臣。而君主也不能随意召见任何人，如果因为一个人见多识广想向他请教问题而召见他，那就像召见自己的老师，是不合礼的。

子思认为国君和贤士存在两个层面的关系：从政治地位来讲，国君是君上，贤士是臣下；从德行和学问来讲，国君是贤士的学生，应该以师礼侍奉贤士。子思和缪公的关系更多侧重于德行方面，孔子和鲁君的关系则侧重于政治行为，这是以入仕与否为标准进行的判断，这也可以让我们更加理解子思和孔子各自不同的做法。招人有道，不以其道招之，虞人死也不敢从命，所以孔子加以赞同。由此，孟子对国君提出了“礼门义路”的进修要求，对待贤士要严格按照礼义之道行事。其实，贤士与国君的关系反映的是德行、知识同政治权利的辩证关系，二者的和谐是社会发展的重要因素。孟子尤其强调士人的人格独立，对当时士人曲意逢迎君主的行为进行反思，挺立起知识分子的脊梁，引导社会真正尊重知识、尊崇德行。

10.8

孟子谓万章曰：“一乡之善士，斯友一乡之善士；一国之善士，斯友一国之善士；天下之善士，斯友天下之善士。以友天下之善士为未足，又尚[1]论古之人。颂[2]其诗，读其书，不知其人，可乎？是以论其世也。是尚友也。”

Mencius said to Wan Zhang, “The scholar whose virtue is most distinguished in a village shall make friends of all the virtuous scholars in the village. The scholar whose virtue is most distinguished throughout a state shall make friends of all the virtuous scholars of that state. The scholar whose virtue is most distinguished throughout the kingdom shall make friends of all the virtuous scholars of the kingdom. When a scholar feels that his friendship with all the virtuous scholars of the kingdom is not sufficient to satisfy him, he proceeds to ascend to consider the men of antiquity. He repeats their poems, and reads their books, and as he does not know what they were as men, to ascertain this, he considers their history. This is to ascend and make friends of the men of antiquity."

【注释】［1］尚：上。［2］颂：吟诵。

【译文】孟子对万章说："一乡中的优秀人物，和这一乡的优秀人物交朋友；一国中的优秀人物，和这一国的优秀人物交朋友；天下的优秀人物，和天下的优秀人物交朋友。假如认为同天下的优秀人物交朋友还不够，那就上溯到古代的人物。吟诵他们的诗，读他们的著作，（但）不了解他们的为人，行吗？所以还要研究他们所处的时代背景。这就是同古人交朋友。"

【解读】本章的中心观念是“尚论古人”和“知人论世”。在一个人的成长过程中，需要结交有共同兴趣和理念的人为友。孔子和孟子都认为，朋友之间切磋沟通、取长补短，这对一个人增益智慧、丰富心灵、开阔眼界都是极为重要的。所以善士应当与善士交游，一乡的优秀人物相互交往，一国的优秀人物相互交往，普天下的优秀人物互相交往，这也切合曾子所说的“君子以文会友，以友辅仁”。如果认为这还不足够，那就跳出时间的局限与古代的善士相交流，从他们那儿汲取营养。为此必须“颂其诗”“读其书”，可要想真正了解写诗著书的人，必须研究他们所处的社会和时代，这就是孟子的“知人论世”说。“知人论世”说对后世的中国文学批评影响深远，直至今日，这一方法也仍在中国学界广泛使用。

10.9

齐宣王问卿。

孟子曰："王何卿之问也？"

王曰："卿不同乎？"

曰："不同。有贵戚之卿[1]，有异姓之卿。"

王曰："请问贵戚之卿。"

曰："君有大过则谏，反覆之而不听，则易位[2]。"

王勃然变乎色。

曰："王勿异也。王问臣，臣不敢不以正[3]对。"

王色定，然后请问异姓之卿。

曰："君有过则谏，反覆之而不听，则去。"

The king Xuan of Qi asked about the *office of* chief ministers.

Mencius said, "Which chief ministers is Your Majesty asking about?"

"Are there differences among them?" inquired the king.

"There are." was the reply. "There are the chief ministers who are noble and relatives *of the prince,* and there are those who are of a different surname."

The king said, "I beg to ask about the chief ministers who are noble and relatives of the prince."

Menciue answered, "If the prince have great faults, they ought to remonstrate with him, and if he do not listen to them after they have done so again and again, they ought to dethrone him."

The king on this loked moved, and changed countenance.

Mencius said, "Let not Your Majesty be offended. You asked me, and I dare not answer but according to truth."

The king's countenance became composed, and he then begged to ask about chief ministers who were of a different surname *from the prince*.

Mencius said, "When the prince has faults, they ought to remonstrate with him, and if he do yot listen to them after they have done this again and again, they ought to leave *the state*."

【注释】［1］贵戚之卿：与异姓之卿对文，指同姓的卿。［2］易位：另立国君。［3］正：诚。

【译文】齐宣王询问（孟子）与公卿相关的问题。

孟子说："大王问哪一种公卿呢？"

齐宣王问："公卿还有不同的吗？"

（孟子）说："不同。有（和国君同宗的）贵戚之卿，有异姓之卿。"

齐宣王说："请问贵戚之卿（应该怎样）。"

（孟子）说："（作为贵戚之卿）国君有了重大错误就要劝谏，反复劝谏还不听，就另立国君。"

齐宣王一下子变了脸色。

（孟子）说："大王不要惊异。大王问我，

我不敢不诚实地回答您。”

齐宣王脸色恢复了正常，然后问异姓之卿（应该怎样）。

（孟子）说：“（作为异姓之臣）国君有过错就要劝谏，反复劝谏而不听，就离开。”

【解读】本章讨论了“贵戚之卿”和“异姓之卿”在国家中的不同政治责任。家天下时代，一国之君也是宗族之君，贵戚之卿是由和国君同宗的亲族来担任，如殷商的箕子、比干，周朝的周公等人。当国君有了重大错误时贵戚之卿可以劝谏，反复劝谏不听就另立国君。异姓之卿是国君有过错时就劝谏，反复劝谏而不听时，就离开。孟子从不主张“愚忠”，相反对国君更多是主张“易位”“诛一夫纣矣”，甚至对国家机器“社稷”也可“变置”。

在孟子看来，国君之位是可以变更的，儒家强调贤者上、能者上，精英治国；如果国君残暴，倒行逆施，那就由贵戚之卿另立

宗族中的贤君。《荀子·臣道》："故谏争辅拂之人，社稷之臣也，国君之宝也，明君之所尊厚也……"其中阐述了不论是宗亲贵族、还是异姓贵族，对无道之君都拥有"谏、争、辅、拂"等权利。"谏"是批评；"争"是以死进谏；"辅"是聚集群臣百官强行纠正君主的过错，"拂"是指暂时代行君权，类似伊尹辅政。孟子认为卿大夫的身份定位不同，承担的职责使命就不一样，这对于国君而言也是一种警醒。

告子上

Gaozi 1

11.1

告子[1]曰："性，犹杞柳[2]也；义，犹桮棬[3]也。以人性为仁义，犹以杞柳为桮棬。"

孟子曰："子能顺杞柳之性而以为桮棬乎？将戕贼[4]杞柳而后以为桮棬也？如将戕贼杞柳而以为桮棬，则亦将戕贼人以为仁义与？率天下之人而祸仁义者，必子之言夫！"

The philosopher Gao said, "Man's nature is like the qi willow, and righteousness is like a cup or a bowl. The fashioning benevolence and righteousness out of man's nature is like the making cups and bowls from the qi willow."

Mencius replied, "Can you, leaving untouched the nature of the willow, make with it cups and bowls? You must do violence and injury to the willow, before you can make cups and bowls with

it. If you must do violence and injury to the willow in order to make cups and bowls with it, on your principles you must in the same way do violence and injury to humanity in order to fashion from it benevolence and righteousness! Your words, alas! would certainly lead all men on to reckon benevolence and righteousness to be calamities."

【注释】[1]告子：战国时期思想家，年龄稍长于孟子，以主张"性无善无不善"的人性论而著称。[2]杞（qǐ）柳：落叶丛生灌木，枝条柔软，可用来编制器物。[3]桮棬（bēi quān）：此处泛指用柳条做成的筐。[4]戕贼：毁伤，残害。

【译文】告子说："人性，好比是杞柳；仁义，好比用柳条做成的筐子。把人性看作是仁义的，就如同把柳条直接当作筐子。"

孟子说："你是顺着杞柳的性状把它做

孟子与告子辩论　吴泽浩 绘

成筐子呢？还是要伤害了它的性状把它做成筐子呢？如果是伤害了它的性状而把它做成筐子，那么也要伤害了人的本性使人变得仁义吗？率领天下的人来祸害仁义的，必定是你这种论调吧！”

【解读】本章孟子与告子辩论，两人通过柳条与柳筐的关系类比说明自己对人性与仁义关系的认识。告子持“无善无不善”论，孟子则持性善论，因此两人进行了多次辩论。告子认为，人之性本来就没有什么仁义，要使人性变得有仁义，就需要改变人性，如同把杞柳编成筐子一样。言下之意就是：人要想有仁义的善性，必须经过后天的改造。而孟子认为，杞柳之所以能做成筐子，是因为它本身就具有相关的性状，而不是违逆其本性做成的。主张违逆本性的人，就会伤害到仁义，因为人性中的仁义是与生俱来的，而不是后天改造的。因此，对待人性不能戕害，而应该采取适宜做法引导其善质本性的自然流露和永久保持。否则，不顾事实的干预就会损害仁义，这也是孟子极力反对的。

11.2

告子曰："性犹湍水[1]也，决诸东方则东流，决诸西方则西流。人性之无分于善不善也，犹水之无分于东西也。"

孟子曰："水信[2]无分于东西，无分于上下乎？人性之善也，犹水之就下也。人无有不善，水无有不下。今夫水，搏[3]而跃之，可使过颡[4]；激[5]而行之，可使在山。是岂水之性哉？其势则然也。人之可使为不善，其性亦犹是也。"

The philosopher Gao said, "Man's nature is like water whirling round in a corner. Open a passage for it to the east, and it will flow to the east; open a passage for it to the west, and it will flow to the west. Man's nature is indifferent to good and evil, just as the water is indifferent to the east and west."

Mencius replied, "Water indeed will flow

indifferently to the east or west, but will it flow indifferently up or down? The tendency of man's nature to good is like the tendency of water to flow downwards. There are none but have this tendency to good, just as all water flows downwards. Now by striking water and causing it to leap up, you may make it go over your forehead, and, by damming and leading it you may force it up a hill; —but are such movements according to the nature of water? It is the force applied which causes them. When men are made to do what is not good, their nature is dealt with in this way."

【注释】［1］湍水：激流。［2］信：确实。［3］搏：拍击。［4］颡（sǎng）：额头。［5］激：堵住水流，使水位提高。

【译文】告子说："人性好比湍急的水流，在东边开个口就往东流，在西边开个口就往西流。人性本来就不分善与不善，就像水流本来不分向东向西一样。”

孟子说：“水流确实是不分向东向西的，难道也不分向上向下吗？人性的善质，就好比水朝下流的性质一样。人性没有不善的，水没有不向下流的。水，拍打一下使它飞溅起来，也能高过人的额头；阻挡住它使其倒流，可以流到山上。这难道是水的本性吗？是形势导致它这样的。人之所以可以变得不善，其中的性质也是这个道理。”

【解读】本章告子把人性比喻成水，水本无方向之分，随着环境的改变而改变，那么人性如水也就没有善与不善之别了。言下之意，就是人本来没有什么善恶分明，遇善趋善，遇恶趋恶。在孟子看来，这种观点显然是难以成立的，水往低处流是水之本性，如同人之本性向善的原理一样，以此肯定了人性向善的合理性。水流之所以发生改变，是受到外界环境的影响。人性也是如此，如果向善的渠道受阻，那么人性就会发生改变，成为不善，甚至成为大恶。当然，人在复杂纷扰的社会之中生存，充满未知，人性在其中也接受着种种考验。

11.3

告子曰："生[1]之谓性。"

孟子曰："生之谓性也，犹白之谓白与？"

曰："然。"

"白羽之白也，犹白雪之白；白雪之白犹白玉之白与？"

曰："然。"

"然则犬之性，犹牛之性；牛之性犹人之性与？"

The philosopher Gao said, "Life is what we call nature."

Mencius asked him, "Do you say that by nature you mean life, just as you say that white is white?"

"Yes, I do," was the reply.

Mencius added, "Is the whiteness of a white feather like that of white snow, and the whiteness of white snow like that of white jade?"

Gao again said, "Yes."

Mencius said, "Very well," pursued Mencius. "Is the nature of a dog like the nature of an ox, and the nature of an ox like the nature of a man?"

【注释】［1］生：天生。

【译文】告子说："天生的属性称作性。"

孟子说："天生的属性称作性，就像所有的白色称作白吗？"

（告子）说："是的。"

（孟子说：）"白羽毛的白，就像白雪的白；白雪的白，就像白玉的白吗？"

（告子）说："是的。"

（孟子说：）"那么，狗性就像牛性，牛性就像人性吗？"

【解读】告子认为，一切事物从诞生那一刻起，无论是生理上还是心理上的东西都是与生俱

来的，都可以称之为“性”。孟子针对这一观点进行了反问式的驳斥。孟子以白色为例，意在强调同为“白”之间的差异，但告子依然坚持己见。孟子进一步问道：“狗性就像牛性，牛性就像人性吗？”告子完全没有意识到同中有异的道理，故而孟子连续追问，致使告子哑口无言了！

本章反映出孟子和告子在人性定义范畴上的分歧，这也是二人辩论的重要起因。告子认为人与生俱来的全部皆可归为人性，而孟子认为所谓人性并非与生俱来的性的全部。

11.4

告子曰："食色[1]，性也。仁，内也，非外也；义，外也，非内也。"

孟子曰："何以谓仁内义外也？"

曰："彼长而我长之[2]，非有长于我也；犹彼白而我白之，从其白于外也，故谓之外也。"

曰："异于[3]白马之白也，无以异于白人之白也；不识长马之长也，无以异于长人之长与？且谓长者义乎？长之者义乎？"

曰："吾弟则爱之，秦人之弟则不爱也，是以我为悦者也，故谓之内。长楚人之长，亦长吾之长，是以长为悦者也，故谓之外也。"

曰："耆[4]秦人之炙[5]，无以异于耆吾炙。夫物则亦有然者也，然则耆炙亦有外与？"

The philosopher Gao said, "To enjoy food and delight in colours is nature. Benevolence is internal and not external; righteousness is external and not internal."

Mencius asked him, "What is the ground of your saying that benevolence is internal and righteousness external?"

He replied, "There is a man older than I, and I give honour to his age. It is not that there is first in me a principle of such reverence to age. It is just as when there is a white man, and I consider him white; —according as he is so externally to me. On this account, I pronounce of righteousness that it is external."

Mencius said, "There is no difference between our pronouncing a white horse to be white and our pronouncing a white man to be white. But is there no difference between the regard with which we acknowledge the age of an old horse and that with which we acknowledge the age of an old man? And what is it which is called righteousness? The fact of a man's being old? Or the fact of our giving honour to his age?"

Gao said, "There is my younger brother; — I love him. But the younger brother of a man of Qin I do not love; that is, the feeling is determined by myself, and therefore I say that benevolence is internal. On the other hand, I give honour to an old man of Chu, and I also give honour to an old man of my own people; that is, the feeling is determined by the age, and therefore I say that righteousness is external."

Mencius answered him, "Our enjoyment of meat roasted by a man of Qin does not differ from our enjoyment of meat roasted by ourselves. Thus, what you insist on takes place also in the case of such things, and will you say likewise that our enjoyment of a roast is external?"

【注释】［1］食色：喜好美食、美色。［2］彼长（zhǎng）而我长之：本句第一个“长”为名词，指年长；第二个“长”为动词，指尊敬。［3］异于：此处疑为衍文。［4］耆：同“嗜”，嗜好。［5］炙（zhì）：烤肉。

【译文】告子说：“喜好美食美色，这是本性的一种体现。仁是产生自内心的，不是由外因引起的；义是外因引起的，不是产生自内心的。”

孟子说：“凭什么说仁是产生自内心而义是外因引起的呢？”

（告子）说：“有人比我年长，我便以长者的礼遇尊敬他，而不是他本来就值得我尊敬；好比某些东西白，我便认为是白，这是从东西白的外表来认识，所以说（义）是外因引起的。”

（孟子）说：“白马的白和白人的白没有什么区别；不知道对老马的尊敬，和对长者的尊敬没有什么区别吗？再说，是认为长者那里存在义呢，还是尊敬他的人那里存在义呢？”

（告子）说：“是我兄弟，我就爱他；是秦国人的兄弟，就不会去爱，这是由我内心的喜好来决定爱谁的，所以说（仁）是生自内心的。尊敬楚国人中的长者，也尊敬我自己国家的长者，这是由对方年长决定的，所以说（义）是外部引起的。”

（孟子）说：“爱吃秦国人的烤肉，同爱吃自己国家的烤肉是没有什么区别的。其他事物也有这种情况，那么爱吃烤肉也是由外因引起的吗？”

【解读】本章中孟子和告子对“仁内义外”的观点进行了辩论。虽然二人都主张“仁”是内在的，但告子主张“义”是外在的，孟子则主张“义”也是内在的。

首先，告子提出“食色，性也”的观点，这和《礼记·礼运》中孔子所云“饮食男女，人之大欲存焉”看似相仿，但实有不同。孔子把食色归为欲望范畴而没有谓之性，告子则直接将食色归为人性，也就是把知觉运动归为人性，其实也是在重申上章“生之谓性”的观点。

其次，孟子和告子通过对“白马”与“白人”、“长马”与“长人”、“爱吾弟”与“爱秦人之弟”、“长楚人之长”与“长吾之长”、“耆秦人之炙”与“耆吾炙”等事项的辨析，以譬喻的方法来表明各自观点。虽然譬喻方法对于理解哲学问题具有辅助作用，但其并不能等同于严密的逻辑论证，所以会显得公说公有理，婆说婆有理。

由于告子和孟子的辩论是收在《孟子》一书里，编撰者笔下的孟子总是比告子略胜一筹，而我们又感觉告子的论证总是未能畅所欲言。总之，告子和孟子的辩论在先秦思想史中具有重要意义，深入认识他们的辩论，对于理解一些哲学问题是大有裨益的。

11.5

孟季子[1]问公都子曰："何以谓义内也？"

曰："行吾敬，故谓之内也。"

"乡人长于伯兄一岁，则谁敬？"

曰："敬兄。"

"酌[2]则谁先？"

曰："先酌乡人。"

"所敬在此，所长在彼，果在外，非由内也。"

公都子不能答，以告孟子。

孟子曰："敬叔父乎？敬弟乎？彼将曰：'敬叔父。'曰：'弟为尸[3]，则谁敬？'彼将曰：'敬弟。'子曰：'恶在[4]其敬叔父也？'彼将曰：'在位故也。'子亦曰：'在位故也。庸[5]敬在兄，斯须[6]之敬在乡人。'"

季子闻之曰："敬叔父则敬，敬弟则敬，果在外，非由内也。"

公都子曰："冬日则饮汤[7]，夏日则饮水，然则饮食亦在外也？"

The disciple Meng Ji asked Gongdu, saying, "On what ground is it said that righteousness is internal?" Gongdu replied, "We therein act out our feeling of respect, and therefore it is said to be internal."

The other objected, "Suppose the case of a villager older than your elder brother by one year, to which of them would you show the greater respect?" "To my brother," was the reply.

"But for which of them would you first pour out wine at a feast?" "For the villager."

Meng Ji argued, "Now your feeling of reverence rests on the one, and now the honour due to age is rendered to the other—this is certainly determined by what is without, and does not proceed from within."

Gongdu was unable to reply, and told the conversation to Mencius.

Mencius said, "You should ask him, 'Which do you respect most, your uncle, or your younger brother?' He will answer, 'My uncle.' Ask him again, 'If your younger brother be personating a dead ancestor, to which do you show the greater respect, to him or to your uncle?' He will say, 'To my younger brother.' You can go on, 'But where is the respect due, as you said, to your uncle?' He will reply to this, 'I show the respect to my younger brother, because of the position which he occupies,' and you can likewise say, 'So my respect to the villager is because of the position which he occupies. Ordinarily, my respect is rendered to my elder brother; for a brief season, on occasion, it is rendered to the villager.' "

Meng Ji heard this and observed, "When respect is due to my uncle, I respect him, and when respect is due to my younger brother, I respect him; the thing is certainly determined by what is without, and does not proceed from within."

Gongdu replied, "In winter we drink things hot, in summer we drink things cold; and so, on your principle, eating and drinking also depend on what is external!"

【注释】[1]孟季子：相传是孟仲子的从兄弟。也有学者认为是任国国君之弟季任。[2]酌：斟酒。[3]尸：古代祭祀时，代死者受祭、象征死者神灵的人，以臣下或死者的晚辈充任。[4]恶（wū）在：出于什么的原因。恶：疑问代词，哪里。[5]庸：平时，平常。[6]斯须：暂时。[7]汤：热水。

【译文】孟季子问公都子说："为什么说义是内在的呢？"

（公都子）说："行为是我敬意的体现，

所以说义是从内心直接发出的。”

（孟季子问：）“有个同乡人比你长兄大一岁，那么应该敬谁？”

（公都子）说：“应该敬长兄。”

（孟季子又问：）“要斟酒的话，先给谁斟？”

（公都子）说：“先给那个同乡人斟酒。”

（孟季子说：）“所要敬的是长兄，斟酒时却因同乡人年长要先给他斟酒，果然还是因为内心之外所面对的人不同，而不是由自己内心直接发出的。”

公都子没有能力回答，就把这事儿告诉了孟子。

孟子说：“应该是敬叔父呢？还是敬弟弟呢？别人会说：‘尊敬叔父。’如果你说：‘弟弟充当了受祭的代理人，那该敬谁？’别人会说：‘敬弟弟。’您如果说：‘出于什么原因敬叔叔呢？’别人会说：‘因为叔父处在叔父的地位上。’您也会说：‘因为弟弟处在充当了受祭人的尸位上。平时所敬的是长兄，这会儿所敬的是同乡人。’”

孟季子听说了这番话，说：“敬叔父是因为他是叔父才表现出敬意，敬弟弟是因为弟弟在尸位才表现出敬意，果然还是因为人所在的地位不同才会有所敬的不同，而不是由内心直接发出的。”

公都子说：“冬天就想喝热水，夏天就想喝凉水，这样的饮食也是由于外在情况不同而引发出来的吗？”

【解读】告子的“义外”论影响很大，就连孟季子也怀疑“义内”说，所以发出了“何以谓义内也”之问。

义，到底是内在的东西还是外在的东西，孟子在上章已经给出了明确答案，但其中的道理未必人人都信。孟季子也是一位善辩高手，他的两问诱导出公都子“敬兄”“先酌乡人”的两个回答，得出了“义外”的定论，使得公都子无言以对。依孟季子的观点：人物的不同，环境的不同，决定着是否会产生敬意。这种逻辑貌似很有道理，也会在生活中经常出现，所以有着很大的迷惑性，但却忽略了这是一种心理反应上的“以心随物”现象。公都子所言“敬兄”“先酌乡人”，是在没有先决条件的情况下说出的，这是一种本能的“以心应物”的现象。

“以心应物”与“以心随物”的区别，就在于一个是“心做主”，一个是“物做主”。所以孟子举了一个特殊环境下的角色转换：“弟为尸”时，应该敬弟，是因为人们从内心感觉到此时弟不为弟，而是受祭者；过后，弟还是弟，完成了“为尸”的使命，人们所敬的还是叔父。此言意在说明人是内心存仁，然后“应物”而成仁义。在平常敬意发自内心不会发生改变，而在特殊情况下敬意会发生改变，但是这种改变并非因“物”引发，而是内心的“应物”而发。公都子明白这个

道理后，立即举了一个非常简单的生活实例来反问孟季子，强调了喝水吃饭此类小事，是内在需要而不是外因所求。

11.6

公都子曰："告子曰：'性无善无不善也。'或曰：'性可以为善，可以为不善；是故文、武兴，则民好善；幽、厉兴，则民好暴。'或曰：'有性善，有性不善；是故以尧为君而有象，以瞽瞍为父而有舜；以纣为兄之子且以为君，而有微子启、王子比干[1]。'今曰'性善'，然则彼皆非与？"

孟子曰："乃若[2]其情，则可以为善矣，乃所谓善也。若夫为不善，非才[3]之罪也。恻隐之心，人皆有之；羞恶之心，人皆有之；恭敬之心，人皆有之；是非之心，人皆有之。恻隐之心，仁也；羞恶之心，义也；恭敬之心，礼也；是非之心，智也。仁义礼智，非由外铄[4]我也，我固有之也，弗思耳矣。故曰：'求则得之，舍则失之。'或相倍蓰[5]而无算者，不能尽其才者也。《诗》[6]曰：'天生蒸[7]民，有物有则[8]。民之秉夷[9]，好是懿[10]德。’孔子曰：‘为此诗者，其知道乎！故有物必有则，民之秉夷也，故好是懿德。’”

The disciple Gongdu said, “The philosopher Gao says, ‘Man’s nature is neither good nor bad.’ Some say, ‘Man’s nature may be made to practise good, and it may be made to practise evil, and accordingly, under Wen and Wu, the people loved what was good, while under Yu and Li, they loved what was cruel.’ Some say, ‘The nature of some is good, and the nature of others is bad. Hence it was that under such a sovereign as Yao there yet appeared Xiang; that with such a father as Gusou there yet appeared Shun; and that with Zhou for their sovereign, and the son of their elder brother besides, there were found Qi, the viscount of Wei, and the prince Bigan.’ And now you say, ‘The nature is good.’ Then are all those wrong?”

Mencius said, “From the feelings proper to it, it is constituted for the practice of what is good.

This is what I mean in saying that the nature is good. If men do what is not good, the blame cannot be imputed to their natural powers. The feeling of commiseration belongs to all men; so does that of shame and dislike; and that of reverence and respect; and that of approving and disapproving. The feeling of commiseration implies the principle of benevolence; that of shame and dislike, the principle of righteousness; that of reverence and respect, the principle of propriety; and that of approving and disapproving, the principle of knowledge. Benevolence, righteousness, propriety, and knowledge are not infused into us from without. We are certainly furnished with them. And a different view is simply owing to want of reflection. Hence it is said, 'Seek and you will find them. Neglect and you will lose them.' Men differ from one another in regard to them; —some as much again as others, some five times as much, and some to an incalculable amount; —it is because they cannot carry out fully their natural powers. It is said in the *Book of Poetry*, 'Heaven in producing mankind, gave them their various faculties and relations with their specific laws. These are the invariable rules of nature for all to hold, and all love this admirable virtue.' Confucius said, 'The maker of this ode knew indeed the principle of our nature!' We may thus see that every faculty and relation must have its law, and since there are invariable rules for all to hold, they consequently love this admirable virtue."

【注释】［1］微子启、王子比干：微子启：据《左传》《史记》记载，是纣王的庶兄，这里微子启是指纣王的伯父或叔父。王子比干：纣王叔父，因劝谏而被纣王剖心而死。［2］乃若：如果说。［3］才：天生之材质。［4］铄（shuò）：融化金属，这里用为“锤炼”之意。［5］倍蓰（xǐ）：数倍之意。倍：一倍。蓰：五倍。［6］《诗》：指《诗经·大雅·烝

孟子与公都子讨论“性善论”　吴磊 绘

民》。[7]蒸：同“烝”，众多。[8]有物：有事情要做。有则：有法则要遵守。[9]秉夷：秉持常性。夷：同“彝”。[10]懿：美。

【译文】公都子说：“告子说过：‘性，无所谓善，也无所谓不善。’有人说：‘性，可以成为善的，也可以成为不善的；所以周文王、周武王得到天下时民众就爱好向善；周幽王、周厉王统治天下时民众就喜好暴力。’有人说：‘有性善的人，有性不善的人；所以（性善的）尧为君主时却有（性不善的）象，以瞽瞍这样坏的父亲却有着（性善的）舜；纣作为（微子、比干）兄弟的儿子，并且以他为君主，却有（性善的）微子启、王子比干。’现在说‘性善’，那么以上所说都是错误的吗？”

孟子说：“如果说人顺应真情，则可以向善，这就是所谓的善。至于有人做出不善的事，那不是天性上的问题。恻隐之心，人人都有；羞恶之心，人人都有；恭敬之心，人人都有；是非之心，人人都有。恻隐之心，可以修养成仁；羞恶之心，可以修养成义；恭敬之心，可以修养成礼；是非之心，可以修养成智。仁、义、礼、智，不是由外在的事物锤炼我所得，而是我本来就具有的，只是人们不去思考这些罢了。所以说：‘求善就能得到，舍弃善就会失去。’有的人（善的积累同别人比）相差一倍、数倍，甚至无法计算，这是因为不能充分发挥自己天生之才的缘故。《诗经》上说：‘上天既然生众民，有事物便有法则。众民秉持其常性，所以爱好其美德。’孔子说：‘作此诗的人，是懂得大道的啊！所以说有事物也一定有法则，众民秉持了常性，所以才会爱好这样的美德。’”

【解读】本章公都子总结出当时除性善论之外的三种人性观：“性无善无不善”“性可以为善，可以为不善”和“有性善，有性不善”。

告子的“性无善无不善”认为人性本来是无所谓善恶的，“性可以为善，可以为不善”是在告子“性白说”的基础上提出人性在后天受外部因素的影响可以趋向于“善”或“不善”，例如受文武二王影响的民众是向善的，而幽厉二王统治下的民众则好暴。这一观点强调了人性的可塑性，故而为教化行为预留了理论前提。

“有性善，有性不善”则认为人天生就有性上的“善”与“不善”之分，而教化与惩罚都是无用的，直接否定了孟子“人人皆可以为尧舜”的论断。要知道，所有这些观点，例证都是在预设前提的情况下发出的。所以，孟子用人与生俱来的恻隐之心、羞恶之心、恭敬之心、是非之心，来辨明人性善的事实，并与自行修养得来仁、义、礼、智的美德相关联。同时引用《诗经》及孔子的语录加以印证：有事物也一定有法则的正常情况下，人有着“好是懿德”的本性。

11.7

孟子曰："富岁，子弟多赖[1]；凶岁，子弟多暴，非天之降才尔殊[2]也，其所以陷溺其心者然也。今夫麰麦[3]，播种而耰[4]之，其地同，树[5]之时又同，浡然[6]而生，至于日至[7]之时，皆熟矣。虽有不同，则地有肥硗[8]，雨露之养，人事之不齐也。故凡同类者，举相似也，何独至于人而疑之？圣人与我同类者。故龙子[9]曰：'不知足而为屦，我知其不为蒉[10]也。'屦之相似，天下之足同也。口之于味，有同耆[11]也。易牙[12]先得我口之所耆者也。如使口之于味也，其性与人殊[13]，若犬马之与我不同类也，则天下何耆皆从易牙之于味也？至于味，天下期于易牙，是天下之口相似也。惟耳亦然。至于声，天下期于师旷，是天下之耳相似也。惟目亦然。至于子都[14]，天下莫不知其姣也。不知子都之姣者，无目者也。故曰：口之于味也，有同耆焉；耳之于声也，有同听焉；目之于色也，有同美焉。至于心，独无所同然乎？心之所同然者何也？谓理也，义也。圣人先得我心之所同然耳。故理义之悦我心，犹刍豢[15]之悦我口。”

Mencius said, “In good years the children of the people are most of them good, while in bad years the most of them abandon themselves to evil. It is not owing to any difference of their natural powers conferred by Heaven that they are thus different. The abandonment is owing to the circumstances through which they allow their minds to be ensnared and drowned in evil. There now is barley. Let it be sown and covered up; the ground being the same, and the time of sowing likewise the same, it grows rapidly up, and, when the full time is come, it is all found to be ripe. Although there may be inequalities of produce, that is owing to the difference of the soil, as rich or poor, to the unequal nourishment afforded by the rains and dews, and to the different ways in which man has performed his business in reference to it. Thus all things which are the same in kind are like to one another; —why should we doubt in regard to man, as if he were a solitary exception to this? The sage and we are the same in kind. In accordance with this the scholar Long said, 'If a man make hempen sandals without knowing the size of people's feet, yet I know that he will not make them like baskets.' Sandals are all like one another, because all men's feet are like one another. So with the mouth and flavours; —all mouths have the same relishes. Yiya only apprehended before me what my mouth relishes. Suppose that his mouth in its relish for flavours differed from that of other men, as is the case with dogs or horses which are not the same in kind with us, why should all men be found following Yiya in their relishes? In the matter of tastes all

the people model themselves after Yiya; that is, the mouths of all men are like one another. And so also it is with the ear. In the matter of sounds, the whole people model themselves after the music-master Kuang; that is, the ears of all men are like one another. And so also it is with the eye. In the case of Zidu, there is no man but would recognise that he was beautiful. Any one who would not recognise the beauty of Zidu must have no eyes. Therefore I say, —Men's mouths agree in having the same relishes; their ears agree in enjoying the same sounds; their eyes agree in recognising the same beauty; —shall their minds alone be without that which the similarly approve? What is it then of which they similarly approve? It is, I say, the principles of our nature, and the determinations of righteousness. The sages only apprehended before me that of which my mind approves along with other men. Therefore the principles of our nature and the determinations of righteousness are agreeable to my mind, just as the flesh of grass and grain-fed animals is agreeable to my mouth."

【注释】［1］赖：仰赖，依靠。这里有“凭借好年成而行善”之意。［2］尔殊：如此不同。尔：如此。殊：不同。［3］麰（móu）麦：大麦。［4］耰（yōu）：本为农具名，此处作动词，指用土覆盖种子。［5］树：动词，种植。［6］浡（bó）然：生机旺盛的样子。［7］日至：即成熟日子的到来。［8］硗（qiāo）：土地坚硬瘠薄。［9］龙子：古代的贤人。［10］蒉（kuì）：草筐。［11］耆（shì）：同“嗜”，爱好。［12］易牙：春秋时齐国最擅烹调的人，齐桓公的宠臣。［13］与人殊：即“人与人殊”之意。［14］子都：春秋时代美男子。［15］刍豢（huàn）：食草家畜称刍，食谷家畜称豢。这里泛指牛羊猪狗之类的肉。

【译文】孟子说："在丰收年，少年子弟多凭借好年成做善事；在灾荒年，少年子弟会为了生存而使用暴力，（这种情况的发生）不是人天生所赋予的资质如此不同，而是由于外部环境将他们的善心陷溺导致的。就大麦来说，播种后用土把种子覆盖好，土地相同，播种时间也一致，它们蓬勃生长，到了成熟的日子，全都成熟了。即使有时候有所不同，那也是因为它们生长的土地有的肥沃、有的坚硬瘠薄，或因雨水滋润的多少不同，或是人们所用功的不同。所以凡是同类的事物，全部是相似的，为什么单独说到人时就怀疑这个道理呢？圣人和我们都是同类的人。所以龙子说：'不知道脚的大小而去做鞋，我断定他不会做出一个草筐来。'鞋的形状相近，是因为天下人脚的形状大致相同。嘴对于味道，有相同的爱好。易牙就是最早知道我们的嘴喜好什么味道的从而获得齐桓公的恩宠。假如嘴对于味道的感觉，人和人不同，就像狗、马与我们不同类一样，那么天下的人怎么都会喜欢易牙调制的味道呢？对于口味，天下的人之所以都期待着易牙，是因为天下人的口味相近。耳朵听声也是这样。对于音乐，天下的人都期待师旷，是因为天下人的耳朵所喜欢听的声音是相近的。眼睛看物也是这样。对于子都来说，天下没有人不知道他的相貌美。如果不知道子都的相貌美，那一定是没有长眼睛的人。所以说，人的口舌对于味道，有相同的嗜好；耳朵对于声音，有相同的嗜好；眼睛对于颜色，有相同的美色嗜好。对于人心，难道唯独没有相同的嗜好吗？人们心中相同的嗜好是什么？就是理、义。圣人早就知道我们的心有相同的嗜好。所以理义能使我们内心喜悦，就像家畜之肉满足我们口味的嗜好一样。”

【解读】孟子在本章的开头先提到“富岁”和“凶岁”人们所表现的不同，是因环境不同而导致，

并不是上天没有赋予他们善心。既然人人都怀着一颗善心，为什么人们所表现出的行为会大相径庭呢？

孟子以种植大麦的例子来进一步解析。孟子认可“人人皆可以为尧舜”，但有的人成为圣贤，有的人是凡人，他认为这与大麦生长环境的不同而结出不同的果实原理是相同的。意在强调善心的种子在成长过程中，受到人文环境、教化与个人修养的影响，所以才会产生人与人之间的差异。上天赋予人们的善心是毋庸置疑的。接着孟子引用龙子的话并举例加以说明这样一个道理：人都有相似的地方，脚如此相似，口感、乐感、美感如此相似，善心亦然。做鞋根据脚的形状，那么做人也要从善心出发。人之善心所表现出的有什么相同的嗜好呢？那就是理义。

人都喜欢理义，因为理义是做人待人的准则，不讲理义而为人，则又与禽兽无异了。但我们的现实经验是，每一个人都有独特的口味爱好、音乐爱好和审美爱好，而并不是所有人都趋向于理和义的。所以孟子的这一论说存在一定问题，他混淆整体状态和个体状态，把整体状态当作每一个个体的必然状态。所以我们应更恰当地说，就像人们大多都认为子都貌美一样，社会大众以整体上讲应当是共同趋向于理和义的。

11.8

孟子曰："牛山[1]之木尝美矣，以其郊于大国[2]也，斧斤伐之，可以为美乎？是其日夜之所息[3]，雨露之所润，非无萌蘖[4]之生焉，牛羊又从而牧之，是以若彼濯濯[5]也。人见其濯濯也，以为未尝有材焉，此岂山之性也哉？虽存乎人者，岂无仁义之心哉？其所以放其良心者，亦犹斧斤之于木也，旦旦而伐之，可以为美乎？其日夜之所息，平旦[6]之气，其好恶与人相近也者几希[7]，则其旦昼[8]之所为，有梏亡[9]之矣。梏之反覆，则其夜气不足以存；夜气不足以存，则其违禽兽不远矣。人见其禽兽也，而以为未尝有才焉者，是岂人之情也哉？故苟得其养，无物不长；苟失其养，无物不消。孔子曰：'操则存，舍则亡；出入无时，莫知其乡[10]。'惟心之谓与？"

Mencius said, "The trees of the Niu mountain were once beautiful. Being situated, however, in the borders of a large state, they were hewn down with axes and bills; —and could they retain their beauty? Still through the activity of the vegetative life day and night, and the nourishing influence of the rain and dew, they were not without buds and sprouts springing forth, but then came the cattle and goats and browsed upon them. To these things is owing the bare and stripped appearance of the mountain, and when people now see it, they think it was never finely wooded. But is this the nature of the mountain? And so also of what properly belongs to man; —shall it be said that the mind of any man was without benevolence and righteousness? The way in which a man loses his proper goodness of mind is like the way in which the trees are denuded by axes and bills. Hewn down day after day, can it—the mind—retain its beauty? But there is a development of its life day and night, and in the calm air of the morning, just between night and day, the mind feels in a degree those desires and aversions which are proper to humanity, but the feeling is not strong, and it is fettered and destroyed by what takes place during the day. This fettering taking place again and again, the restorative influence of the night is not sufficient to preserve the proper goodness of the mind; and when this proves insufficient for that purpose, the nature becomes not much different from that of the irrational animals, and when people now see it, they think that it never had those powers which I assert. But does this condition represent the feelings proper to humanity? Therefore, if it receive its proper nourishment, there is nothing which will not grow. If it lose its proper nourishment, there is nothing which will not decay away. Confucius said, 'Hold it fast, and it remains with you. Let it go, and you lose it. Its outgoing and incoming cannot be defined as to time or place.' It is the mind of which this is said!"

【注释】［1］牛山：齐国临淄郊外的山名。［2］郊于大国：在临淄的城外。临淄不仅是齐国的首都，也是当时的大都市之一。［3］息：生长，滋生。［4］萌蘖（niè）：嫩芽新枝。［5］濯濯（zhuó）：没有草木，光秃秃的样子。［6］平旦：黎明，天刚亮时。［7］几希：几乎很少。希：同"稀"。［8］旦昼：白天。［9］有梏（gù）亡：又因受到阻塞而失去。有：同"又"。［10］莫知其乡：难以知道心居于何处。乡：通"向"。

【译文】孟子说："牛山的树木曾经很茂美，但是由于它在大都市的郊外，经常遭到斧子的砍伐，那还能够保持它的茂美吗？即便如此，山上的树木也会日夜都在生长，接受雨露的滋润，不是没有新枝嫩芽再生长出来，但随即又有牛羊被赶着到此放牧，所以也就

像这样光秃秃的了。人们看到山上光秃秃的样子，就认为这里不曾有过成材的树木，这种说法难道符合山的本性吗？即使在那些失去良心的人身上，难道当初就没有仁义之心吗？那些放任良心失去的人，原因也像用斧头砍伐树木一样，天天砍伐，还可以保持茂美吗？人们每个日夜都在生长，在天刚亮时都会有清纯之气，可是一个人心里所产生出来的喜好和厌恶与一般人相近的却很少，那是因为白天的所作所为阻塞了他的清纯之气，所以最终又因受到阻塞失去了他的清纯之气。反复阻塞的结果，便使他们夜晚培养的清纯之气不足以保存下来；夜晚培养的清纯之气不足以保存下来，也就离禽兽不远了。人们见到某人的所作所为近于禽兽，就认为他不曾有过上天赋予的善性，这难道是人的真性情吗？所以说，假如能得到培养，就没有什么东西不会生长；假如失去培养，就没有什么东西不会消亡。孔子说：‘坚持住就能得以保存，放弃掉就会消亡；存与亡没有一定的时候，也不知道它在何方。’这就是指人心而言的吧？”

【解读】本章孟子阐述了“夜息”的道理，以此寓意人在静闲之时能修养心性。说明善良的本性是需要长期养护的，只有不断加强个人修养，才能保持一颗善心的本性。孟子认为，人的善心本性，经过“夜息”的培养，如同天刚亮时的清纯之气。孟子首先以牛山为例，没有人为干扰的牛山，其自然生长的树木非常茂美，寓意人之本性是善的；由于人们砍伐、放牧，牛山变得光秃，比喻人之善良性在外事外物一再的摧残下，会逐渐丧失。当一座牛山的植被被蚕食殆尽时，能说牛山原本就没有树木吗？当一个人的善性消失时，能说明此人从来就没有善性吗？孟子以山为例，非常生动形象，故而很有说服力。任何人都有善良的本性，只不过被外在的事物不断摧残而渐渐丧失，如果不注重个人的修养，就会逐渐脱离人的轨迹，加入禽兽的行列。现实生活中，有的人不注意修养，因而极容易受到外界事物的影响，进而丧失善心善性。如何才能去养护善良的本性呢？这就需要养浩然之气，避污浊习气，祛自私自利。我们应时刻保持善心，让仁义之心永存。

11.9

孟子曰："无或乎王[1]之不智也。虽有天下易生之物也，一日暴[2]之，十日寒之，未有能生者也。吾见亦罕矣，吾退而寒之者至矣，吾如有萌焉何哉[3]？今夫弈之为数[4]，小数也；不专心致志，则不得也。弈秋，通国之善弈者也。使弈秋诲二人弈，其一人专心致志，惟弈秋之为听。一人虽听之，一心以为有鸿鹄[5]将至，思援弓缴[6]而射之，虽与之俱学，弗若之矣。为是其智弗若与？曰：非然也。"

Mencius said, "It is not to be wondered at that the king is not wise! Suppose the case of the most easily growing thing in the world; —if you let it have one day's genial heat, and then expose it for ten days to cold, it will not be able to grow. It is but seldom that I have an audience of the king, and when I retire, there come all those who act upon him like the cold. Though

I succeed in bringing out some buds of goodness, of what avail is it? Now chess-playing is but a small art, but without his whole mind being given, and his will bent, to it, a man cannot succeed at it. Chess Qiu is the best chess-player in all the kingdom. Suppose that he is teaching two men to play. The one gives to the subject his whole mind and bends to it all his will, doing nothing but listening to Chess Qiu. The other, although he seems to be listening to him, has his whole mind running on a swan which he thinks is approaching, and wishes to bend his bow, adjust the string to the arrow, and shoot it. Although he is learning along with the other, he does not come up to him. Why? Because his intelligence is not equal? Not so."

【注释】［1］或：通“惑”，疑惑、怀疑。王：指齐王。［2］暴（pù）：同“曝”，用强烈阳光照晒。［3］吾如有萌焉何哉：我对于齐王随时萌生的新想法又能怎么办呢？意思是无能为力。如……何：古汉语固定句式，意思是“对……怎么办”。[4]弈：围棋。为数：作为一种技艺。[5]鸿鹄：天鹅。[6]援弓缴（zhuó）：手持弓与带绳的箭。缴：系在箭上的丝绳，此处代指箭。

【译文】孟子说：“不要怀疑齐王的智慧不够。即使有一种天下最容易生长的植物，如果晒它一天，却又冻它十天，是没有什么能够生长的。我和齐王相见的机会也是很少的，我一离开齐王，那些给他吹冷风的人就会来了，他如果分心有了新的想法，我有什么办法呢？就拿下围棋作为一种技艺来说，只是一种不难学的小技艺；如果不专心致志地学习，也是不能得其要领的。弈秋，是全国中最擅长下围棋的人。让弈秋同时教两个人下围棋，其中一人能够专心致志，一心聆听弈秋的教诲；另一个虽然也在听，但满心所想的却是有天鹅将要飞来，想着张弓搭箭把它射下来。

虽然这两人都跟随弈秋学习，后者却比不上前者。难道是因为后者的智慧不如前者吗？回答说：不是这样的。”

【解读】本章孟子指出实施“王道”的关键在于君主的坚守。他首先指出，齐王并非智慧不够，而是不能做到始终如一。明确齐宣王要坚定实行王道的信念，不要三心二意，更不要被其他歪理邪说所迷惑。孟子用“一曝十寒”的道理，说明做事情要坚持，要保持一贯性。彼时，齐国设有“稷下学宫”，是各种学派的汇集之地，它们不时地影响着齐国的政治走向，实行“霸道”还是“王道”，到齐宣王时依然摇摆不定。孟子劝齐宣王实行王道，但是孟子离开齐王后，齐王身边多为霸道之臣，齐王听信谗言节外生枝走向歧路。孟子接着又以学习下棋的故事作比，意在告诉人们做任何事情都应该专心致志、心无旁骛，坚持自己正确的信念，不忘初心，一往无前。

11.10

孟子曰："鱼，我所欲也；熊掌，亦我所欲也，二者不可得兼，舍鱼而取熊掌者也。生，亦我所欲也；义，亦我所欲也，二者不可得兼，舍生而取义者也。生亦我所欲，所欲有甚于生者，故不为苟得也；死亦我所恶，所恶有甚于死者，故患有所不辟[1]也。如使人之所欲莫甚于生，则凡可以得生者，何不用也？使人之所恶莫甚于死者，则凡可以辟患者，何不为也？由是[2]则生而有不用也，由是则可以辟患而有不为也。是故所欲有甚于生者，所恶有甚于死者，非独贤者有是心也，人皆有之，贤者能勿丧耳。一箪食，一豆[3]羹，得之则生，弗得则死。呼尔而与之[4]，行道之人弗受；蹴尔而与之[5]，乞人不屑[6]也。万钟则不辨礼义而受之，万钟于我何加焉？为宫室之美、妻妾之奉、所识穷乏者得我与[7]？乡[8]为身死而不受，今为宫室之美为之；乡为身死而不受，今为妻妾之奉为之；乡为身死而不受，今为所识穷乏者得我而为之，是亦不可以已乎？此之谓失其本心。”

Mencius said, “I like fish, and I also like bear's paws. If I cannot have the two together, I will let the fish go, and take the bear's paws. So, I like life, and I also like righteousness. If I cannot keep the two together, I will let life go, and choose righteousness. I like life indeed, but there is that which I like more than life, and therefore, I will not seek to possess it by any improper ways. I dislike death indeed, but there is that which I dislike more than death, and therefore there are occasions when I will not avoid danger. If among the things which man likes there were nothing which he liked more than life, why should he not use every means by which he could preserve it? If among the things which man dislikes there were nothing which he disliked more than death, why should he not do everything by which he could avoid danger? There are cases when men by a certain course might preserve life, and they do not employ it; when by certain things they might avoid danger, and they will not do them. Therefore, men have that which they like more than life, and that which they dislike more than death. They are not men of distinguished talents and virtue only who have this mental nature. All men have it; what belongs to such men is simply that they do not lose it. Here are a small basket of rice and a platter of soup, and the case is one in which the getting them will preserve life, and the want of them will be death; —if they are offered with an insulting voice, even a tramper will not receive them, or if you first tread upon them, even a beggar will not stoop to take them. And yet a man will accept of ten thousand *zhong*, without any consideration of propriety or righteousness. What can the ten thousand *zhong* add to him? When he takes them, is it not that he may obtain beautiful mansions, that he may secure the services of wives and concubines, or that the poor and needy of his acquaintance may be helped by him? In the former case the offered bounty was not received, though it would have saved from death, and now the emolument is taken for the sake of beautiful mansions. The bounty that would have preserved from death was not received, and the emolument is taken to get the service of wives and concubines. The bounty that would have saved from death was not received, and the emolument is taken that one's poor and needy acquaintance may be helped by him. Was it then not possible likewise to decline this? This is a case of what is called —'Losing the proper nature of one's mind.'"

【注释】［1］辟：同"避"。［2］由是：（承接前语）按照人的本心。［3］豆：古代盛羹

孟子论“生与义”的关系　杨文森 绘

汤的器具。［4］呼（hū）尔而与之：大声地呵斥着给人东西。［5］蹴（cù）尔而与之：以脚践踏后给人。［6］不屑：认为不值得，鄙视。［7］所识穷乏者得我与：让所认识的贫穷者感激我的恩惠吗。得：同“德”。与：通“欤”。［8］乡：通“向”，从前。

【译文】孟子说：“鱼，是我想要得到的，熊掌，也是我想要得到的；如果两者不能同时得到，就舍弃鱼而取得熊掌。生存，是我想要得到的，正义，也是我想要得到的；如果两者不能同时得到，就舍弃生存而取其正义。生存也是我想要的，因为所想要得到的还有比生存更重要的，所以就不会苟且获取生存；死亡是我厌恶的，因为所厌恶的事情还有比死亡更严重的，所以即使遇到祸患的时候也不会逃避。如果让人想要得到的没有比生存更重要的，那么，只要是能够生存，还有什么事情不敢做呢？如果让人厌恶的事情没有比死亡更严重的，那么只要能够逃避死亡，还有什么事情不敢做呢？按照人的本心虽然有可以使人生存的办法却不用，按照人的本心虽然有可以使人逃避祸患的办法却不为所动。因此人们想要的有时比生存更重要，所厌恶的有时比死亡更严重，并非只有贤人才有这种本心，而是人人都有，只不过贤人能够保持它罢了。一篮饭，一碗汤，得到便可以活下去，得不到就会死亡。如果大声地呵斥着给人东西吃，过路的人虽然饿着肚子也不会接受；如果用脚踢过去给人吃，就是乞丐也会不屑一顾。非常优厚的俸禄却不分辨是否合乎礼义就接受了，优厚的俸禄对我来说能给我增加什么呢？难道为了住宅的华丽、妻妾的奉养、让所认识的穷苦人感激我的恩惠吗？从前宁肯死去都不接受的事情，现在竟然会为了住宅的华丽而接受了；过去宁肯死去都不接受的事情，现在竟然为了妻妾的奉养而接受了；过去宁肯死去都不接受的做法，

现在竟然为了让所认识的穷苦人感激我的恩惠而去做，这样的情况难道就不能不去做吗？这样做了叫作丧失了本心。”

【解读】本章孟子以“鱼和熊掌”的选择，引生出“生与义”的抉择，目的是强调人“舍生取义”的高尚节操。

“鱼和熊掌”的问题，对于任何人而言都是难以抉择的，它们是人们在生活中难以抵制的诱惑，这似乎只是“小节”。但“生与义”的抉择，却折射出人性的怯懦与光辉。一般情况下，人们往往都会兼顾“生与义”，这是人的“本心”所致，但在不能两全其美的关键时刻是难以抉择的。抉择的不同，反映“义”在个人心中的分量，也反映个人的心性修养。有的人选择义，是因为他知道“为人在于义”的道理，这是“志士”的表现。反之，为生而舍义，如同没有灵魂的行尸走肉，这是懦夫的表现。孟子在这里并没有否定人的求生欲望有着天然的合理性，但既然上天注定人之所以为人，而不是禽兽，那么就应该秉承人之本心去面对一切。也就是说，人就应该以“人心”做人事、行人道，如此所表现出的就是“义”。

在孟子看来，“义”的价值意义远比生存要高贵得多，苟且偷生，枉为其人。不义者，为了能够生存，可能无恶不作；为了避免死亡的祸患，就不会考虑人生的价值。他们没有礼义廉耻，不讲仁义道德。人只有守住本心，才能做出不违背“义”甚至“舍生取义”的举动，才能在人生的旅途中写出一个大大的“人”字。

11.11

孟子曰："仁，人心也；义，人路也。舍其路而弗由[1]，放[2]其心而不知求，哀哉！人有鸡犬放，则知求之；有放心，而不知求。学问之道无他，求其放心而已矣。"

Mencius said, "Benevolence is man's mind, and righteousness is man's path. How lamentable is it to neglect the path and not pursue it, to lose this mind and not know to seek it again! When men's fowls and dogs are lost, they know to seek for them again, but they lose their mind, and do not know to seek for it. The great end of learning is nothing else but to seek for the lost mind."

【注释】［1］弗由：不遵循。［2］放：放弃，失去。

【译文】孟子说："仁，是人的心；义，是人的路。舍弃了这条路不走，放弃了心而不知道寻求，真是悲哀啊！人们如果有鸡、狗丢失了，都知道设法找回；有的人心失去了，却不知道去寻求。学问的正道没有别的门路，不过就是设法找到失去的本心罢了。"

【解读】本章孟子把"仁义"进行了既形象又简单的解说，指出"仁"是人人都天生具有的"人心"；"义"是人人都应该行走的"人路"。言下之意，就是人不失去"仁心"，方可称之为人；人具有了"义"，才可以不失去人生的价值。这里孟子强调了"仁义"对于做人的基本要求，意在说明人与禽兽的区别。如果人心丢失了，没有了"仁"，将人不为人，"义"也就无从谈起，还有什么比这更可悲的事情吗？孟子在这里怀着一颗仁慈之心加以惋惜。所以，人心（仁）是不能丢失的，即便是有时丢失也要设法找回，这是做人的原则。找回人心（仁）的方法只有一条路可走，那就是通过正道的学问寻之且守之，使之归向本善。

从本章我们可以看出孟子的人性论逻辑，孟子以为人性本善，只是有时善良的本心会因不加保持而流失，这个时候孟子又提出了“求其放心”的修养方法论，指导人们注意修养自身而找回并保持善性。

11.12

孟子曰："今有无名之指，屈而不信[1]，非疾痛害事也，如有能信之者，则不远秦、楚之路，为指之不若[2]人也。指不若人，则知恶之；心不若人，则不知恶，此之谓不知类[3]也。"

Mencius said, "Here is a man whose fourth finger is bent and cannot be stretched out straight. It is not painful, nor does it incommode his business, and yet if there be any one who can make it straight, he will not think the way from Qin to Chu far to go to him; because his finger is not like the finger of other people. When a man's finger is not like those of other people, he knows to feel dissatisfied, but if his mind be not like that of other people, he does not know to feel dissatisfaction. This is called —'Ignorance of the relative importance of things.'"

【注释】［1］信：通“伸”。［2］若：及，如。［3］不知类：不知轻重，有“舍本逐末”之意。

【译文】孟子说：“如果现在有个人无名指弯曲而不能伸直，虽然既不疼痛又不妨碍做事，但只要有人能使它伸直，即使赶到秦国、楚国去医治也不嫌远，为的是手指不如别人。手指不如别人，知道厌恶它；心不如别人，却不知道厌恶，这叫不知轻重。”

【解读】孟子在本章中讲了一个人人都有的“心理疾病”，那就是暴露在外的生理缺陷，人们往往会不遗余力地加以修饰矫正，这是人们有着一种本能的羞耻之心所致。这种现象，在我们的现实生活中太常见到了，不必多解。然而，隐藏在体内、外人所不能直视的“心不若人”，反而不觉得羞耻。也就是说，自己的人心（仁）丢失，道德修养、思想境界不如别人，反倒是视而不见，毫无羞愧之感。

这就丧失了“人本”，丢掉了“人之所以为人”的原则。孟子在这里意在呼唤人们，要知道人之本，不可舍本逐末。

11.13

孟子曰："拱把[1]之桐梓，人苟欲生之，皆知所以养之者。至于身，而不知所以养之者，岂爱身不若桐梓哉？弗思甚也。"

Mencius said, "Anybody who wishes to cultivate the *tong* or the *zi,* which may be grasped with both hands, perhaps with one, knows by what means to nourish them. In the case of their own persons, men do not know by what means to nourish them. Is it to be supposed that their regard of their own persons is inferior to their regard for a *tong* or *zi*? Their want of reflection is extreme."

【注释】［1］拱：双手合握。把：把握。

【译文】孟子说："双手可围的桐树梓树，人们要想让它们很好地生长，都知道该怎样去养护。至于自己的身体，反倒不知道应该怎样保养，难道爱自身的成长还不如对桐树、梓树的养护吗？实在是不肯思考问题了。”

【解读】上一章讲到的是“心”，本章孟子讲的是“身”，身心一体，无论是心还是身，都是指培养人的内在品质，也就是“修身养心”或者说“修身养性”。这里孟子之所以用“养身”，主要是以身与桐树、梓树做一形象的比喻。无论是什么树木，要想使其成长为栋梁之材，都需要精心的养护。人的身心成长、不失本真，更加需要不断地加强修养。孟子虽然没有告诉人们如何修养身心，但实例举证更能引发自觉者与不自觉者的思考。知道养树而不注重养身，这实在是舍本逐末，但也确实是大多数人的情况，这不得不让我们产生警惕，时常提醒自己不忘自身。

11.14

孟子曰："人之于身也，兼所爱。兼所爱，则兼所养也。无尺寸之肤不爱焉，则无尺寸之肤不养也。所以考其善不善者，岂有他哉？于己取之而已矣。体有贵贱，有小大。无以小害大，无以贱害贵。养其小者为小人，养其大者为大人。今有场师，舍其梧檟[1]，养其樲棘[2]，则为贱场师焉。养其一指而失其肩背，而不知也，则为狼疾[3]人也。饮食之人，则人贱之矣，为其养小以失大也。饮食之人无有失也，则口腹岂适[4]为尺寸之肤哉？"

Mencius said, "There is no part of himself which a man does not love, and as he loves all, so he must nourish all. There is not an inch of skin which he does not love, and so there is not an inch of skin which he will not nourish. For examining whether his way of nourishing be good or not, what other rule is there but this, that he determine by reflecting on himself where it should be applied? Some parts of the body are noble, and some ignoble; some great, and some small. The great must not be injured for the small, nor the noble for the ignoble. He who nourishes the little belonging to him is a little man, and he who nourishes the great is a great man. Here is a plantation keeper, who neglects his *wu* and *jia,* and cultivates his sour jujube-trees; —he is a poor plantation keeper. He who nourishes one of his fingers, neglecting his shoulders or his back, without knowing that he is doing so, is a man who resembles a hurried wolf. A man who only eats and drinks is counted mean by others; —because he nourishes what is little to the neglect of what is great. If a man, fond of his eating and drinking, were not to neglect what is of more importance, how should his mouth and belly be considered as no more than an inch of skin?"

【注释】[1]梧：梧桐。檟（jiǎ）：楸树的别称。[2]樲（èr）：酸枣树。棘：荆棘。[3]狼疾：同“狼藉”，昏乱，糊涂。[4]适：通“啻”（chì），仅仅，只。

【译文】孟子说：“人对于自己的身体，每个部分都要爱惜。都爱护，便都保养。没有尺寸间的肌肤不爱惜，便没有尺寸间的肌肤不保养。所以考察他护养得好不好，难道有其他方法吗？不过是看他注重身体的哪一部分罢了。身体有重要的部位和次要的部位，它们有小有大。不要因为小的而损害大的，不要因为次要部位而损害重要的部位。着重于护养小部分的是小人，着重于护养大部分的是大人。如果有一位园艺师，舍弃梧桐、楸树，却去培养酸枣、荆棘，那就是一位很糟糕的园艺师。如果有人为护养一根手指而不顾肩背的护养，自己还不明白其中因小失大的道理，那他便是个糊涂之人。那种只知道吃喝的人之所以被人鄙视，就因为他贪小而失大。如果说吃喝并没有失去什么的话，那么口腹难道仅仅是为了护养那尺寸间的肌肤吗？”

【解读】孟子在本章以身体的“小”和“大”，来阐释怎样“养身”的道理。其实，人的每个器官都可以称之为“小”，唯有人的心境为“大”。虽然孟子在这里没有明确指出，但如果细细品味，“大”当指养护“美好品德、高尚道德”的“心”之大。这就是“养其小者为小人，养其大者为大人”之所指。孟子在这里告诉我们，因小失大，如同一位糟糕的园艺师舍贵取贱；如同一位只是知道吃喝之人，为了口腹之需而“饱食终日，无所用心”。人，应该像爱护自己的每一寸肌肤一样进行全面修养，而不应仅仅为了满足口腹之欲而简单地生存。否则，与禽兽又有什么区别？人，不能像“饮食之人”那样养小失大，否则就失去了做人的意义。

11.15

公都子问曰："钧[1]是人也，或为大人，或为小人，何也？"

孟子曰："从[2]其大体[3]为大人，从其小体[4]为小人。"

曰："钧是人也，或从其大体，或从其小体，何也？"

曰："耳目之官[5]不思，而蔽于物，物交物[6]，则引之而已矣。心之官则思，思则得之，不思则不得也。此天之所与我者，先立乎其大者，则其小者弗能夺也。此为大人而已矣。"

The disciple Gongdu said, "All are equally men, but some are great men, and some are little men; — how is this?"

Mencius replied, "Those who follow that part of themselves which is great are great men; those who follow that part which is little are little men."

Gongdu pursued, "All are equally men, but some follow that part of themselves which is great, and some follow that part which is little; —how is this?"

Mencius answered, "The senses of hearing and seeing do not think, and are obscured by external things. When one thing comes into contact with another, as a matter of course it leads it away. To the mind belongs the office of thinking. By thinking, it gets the right view of things; by neglecting to think, it fails to do this. These—the senses and the mind—are what Heaven has given to us. Let a man first stand fast in the supremacy of the nobler part of his constitution, and the inferior part will not be able to take it from him. It is simply this which makes the great man."

【注释】[1]钧：同"均"。[2]从：循，随。[3]大体：心志。[4]小体：耳目口腹之欲。[5]

官：器官，官能。［6］物交物：第一个“物”指外物，第二个“物”指耳目之官。交：接触。

【译文】公都子问道：“同样是人，有的成了君子，有的成了小人，是什么原因？”

孟子说：“能依从重要器官的就成为君子，依从次要器官的就成为小人。”

（公都子）又问：“同样是人，有人能依从重要器官，有人却依从次要器官，为什么呢？”

（孟子）说：“耳朵、眼睛这些器官不会思考，容易被外物蒙蔽，因此一与外物接触，就被引诱过去。心这个器官是会思考的，思考就会有所得，不思考就得不到。这是上天赋予我们的，所以要先树立起来这个重要器官，那么其他次要器官就不会被外物的引诱夺走了。这就是成为君子的道理罢了。”

【解读】本章作为上一章内容的延续与补充，

明确指出了“心”为体之“大”者，两章连读，体的“小”“大”所指便清楚了。“君子”与“小人”的形成，就在于“养大与养小、从大与从小”的区别。既然“心”为体之大、之贵，那么就需要首先修养心性，树立“心”的统领地位。只有“心”得其正，没有思考能力的诸如耳目之属才能不被外事外物所引诱。这里我们必须明白，由于认识事物的历史局限性，古人所谓“心有所思”，是认为心具有思考能力，它能够明是非、辨黑白，知美丑、善恶，而这其实是大脑的功能。所以孟子在本章特别强调对心的重视，“思则得之，不思则不得”一语，更是突显了“心”之思考对于人的重要性。在孟子看来，人之所以能思考、会思考，这是上天特意赋予人类的一种独有功能。与前几章贯通领会，可感悟到孟子依然还是强调人与禽兽之间的区别，意在引起人们对养心的重视。

11.16

孟子曰："有天爵[1]者，有人爵[2]者。仁义忠信，乐善不倦，此天爵也；公卿大夫，此人爵也。古之人修其天爵，而人爵从之。今之人修其天爵，以要[3]人爵；既得人爵，而弃其天爵，则惑之甚者也，终亦必亡而已矣。"

Mencius said, "There is a nobility of Heaven, and there is a nobility of man. Benevolence, righteousness, self-consecration, and fidelity, with unwearied joy in these virtues; —these constitute the nobility of Heaven. To be a *gong*, a *qing*, or a *dafu*; —this constitutes the nobility of man. The men of antiquity cultivated their nobility of Heaven, and the nobility of man came to them in its train. The men of the present day cultivate their nobility of Heaven in order to seek for the nobility of man, and when they have obtained that, they throw away the other: —their delusion is extreme. The issue is simply this, that they must lose that nobility of man as well."

【注释】［1］天爵：天赠的爵位。指因有高尚的道德修养而受人尊敬，无须由人委任赏封。

［2］人爵：指世俗社会由人委任赏封的爵位。

［3］要：通“邀”，求取，追求。

【译文】孟子说：“有天赐的爵位，有人授的爵位。仁义忠信，乐于行善道而不厌倦，这是天赐的爵位；公卿大夫，这是人授的爵位。古代的人修养天赐的爵位，自然而然地就获得人授的爵位了。现在的人修养天赐的爵位，是为了获取人授的爵位；一旦得到人授的爵位，就丢弃天赐的爵位，这实在是太糊涂了，最终连人授的爵位也一定会丧失的。”

【解读】孟子在本章讲“天爵”与“人爵”。

所谓的“天爵”，是通过内心的修炼自然而得，这是精神层次的爵位，也就是精神上的贵族。他们乐施好善、人格高贵，不为物质利益所左右，以精神的满足为最高追求。这种人往往以其人格魅力赢得众人的尊敬、爱戴与拥护，无须由某个人前来委任或赏封，孟子把这种“民选”现象比拟为“天爵”。这里也体现出儒家“天权民授”的思想。孟子之所以把“古之人修其天爵，而人爵从之”与“今之人修其天爵，以要人爵”加以比对，是在感叹物质利益的诱惑使得人之本心逐渐迷失。假如人变得越来越逐利、越来越世俗，不单是人的“天爵”品质丧失殆尽，就连“人爵”应有的可贵之处也会丧失。这也是我们今天应该警醒的问题：人，不要迷失做人的方向。

11.17

孟子曰："欲贵者，人之同心也。人人有贵于己者，弗思耳。人之所贵者，非良贵也。赵孟[1]之所贵，赵孟能贱之。《诗》云[2]：'既醉以酒，既饱以德。'言饱乎仁义也，所以不愿人之膏粱之味也[3]；令闻广誉施于身[4]，所以不愿人之文绣[5]也。"

Mencius said, "To desire to be honored is the common mind of men. And all men have in themselves that which is *truly* honorable. Only they do not think of it. The honor which men confer is not good honor. Those whom Zhao the Great ennobles he can make mean *again*. It is said in the *Book of Poetry*, 'He has filled us with his wine; he has satiated us with his goodness.' '*Satiated us with his goodness,*' that is, satiated us with benevolence and righteousness, and he who is so, consequently, does not wish for the fat meat and fine millet of men. A good reputation and farreaching praise fall to him, and he does not desire the elegant embroidered garments of men."

【注释】[1]赵孟：春秋时期晋国执政大臣赵盾，字孟。此处可以理解为有权势者。[2]《诗》云：出自《诗经·大雅·既醉》。[3]愿：羡慕。膏：肥肉。粱：精米。[4]令：善。闻：与誉同，名望、荣誉。[5]文绣：绣有花纹的官服。

【译文】孟子说："想要得到尊贵，是人们共同的心愿。人人其实都有可尊之处，只是平时不去想到它罢了。别人所给予的尊贵，并不是真正的尊贵。赵孟给予了一个人尊贵，赵孟也能使他低贱。《诗经》上说：'既供奉美酒使他陶醉，又献上仁德使他满足。'这是说仁义满足了，所以就不羡慕别人的美味佳肴了；美好的名声、广泛的赞誉落在自己身上了，所以就不羡慕别人的锦绣衣裳了。”

【解读】在本章中孟子讲到“人人有贵于己者”，就是说人要善于发现自己的可贵之处，并认识其存在的价值。“赵孟之所贵，赵孟能贱之”，是强调了自贵的重要性，因为别人给予的尊贵是可以随时被剥夺的，只有自贵是别人拿不走的。

那么，什么是“人之所贵”，什么是“己贵”呢？就本章下文而言，“膏粱”“文绣”是为“人之所贵”；与之相对应的“仁义”“令闻广誉”是为“己贵”。两者一个是外在的物质，一个是内在的品质，虽然它们都有着尊贵的属性，但本质却不同。功名利禄的大富大贵是别人给予的，有可能一夜之间化为乌有，不再属于自己；而仁义道德，是靠自己修养得来的，才是真正属于自己的，谁也拿不走，谁也无法收回。所以孟子说“人之所贵者，非良贵也”，意在告诉人们：自贵才是真正的尊贵，要想自贵，唯有自己修养仁义道德。这启示我们应当坚守社会良知，抵御利益诱惑。

11.18

孟子曰："仁之胜不仁也，犹水胜火。今之为仁者，犹以一杯水救一车薪之火也；不熄，则谓之水不胜火，此又与[1]于不仁之甚者也，亦终必亡而已矣。"

Mencius said, "Benevolence subdues its opposite just as water subdues fire. Those, however, who nowadays practise benevolence *do it* as if with one cup of water they could save a whole waggon-load of fuel which was on fire, and when the flames were not extinguished, were to say that water cannot subdue fire. This conduct, moreover, greatly encourages those who are not benevolent. The final issue will simply be this—the loss *of that small amount of benevolence*."

【注释】［1］与：助。

【译文】孟子说："仁胜过不仁，就像水可以灭火一样。但现在奉行仁道的人，就像用一杯水去灭一车柴草所燃烧的大火一样；火不熄灭，就说是水不能够灭火，这样的说法正好更加助长了那些不仁的人，结果连他们原本奉行的一点仁道最终也必然会失去。"

【解读】孟子始终坚信"仁者"的力量，认为正义、善良的仁者，一定能够战胜世间的不仁。孟子在这里强调对"仁"的信念不可动摇，虽然只是"杯水车薪"，也当全力以赴奉献自己的微薄之力，这就是"天将降大任于是人也"的豪迈。

孟子在这里用"杯水车薪"来形容"仁与不仁"的较量，可见彼时糟糕的社会现状。故而，孟子竭尽全力呼唤"仁者"的回归，关注"仁者"的不亡。当今社会，我们更应该坚持正义，坚持原则，坚持本真，坚信正义一定能战胜邪恶，为坚守这些亘古不变的真理付出自己的汗水，贡献自己的智慧。

11.19

孟子曰："五谷[1]者，种之美者也；苟为不熟，不如荑稗[2]。夫仁亦在乎熟之而已矣。"

Mencius said, "Of all seeds the best are the five kinds of grain, yet if they be not ripe, they are not equal to the *ti* or the *bai*. So, the value of benevolence depends entirely on its being brought to maturity."

【注释】［1］五谷：泛指各种主要的谷物。多认为是指稻、黍、稷、麦、菽五类。［2］荑稗（tí bài）：两种草名，即秕谷和稗子。荑：通"稊"。

【译文】孟子说："五谷是粮食作物中的好品种，但如果不成熟，那还不如稊稗结出的种子。

仁也就在于使它成熟罢了。”

【解读】孟子在本章之所以用五谷来喻仁，意在说明仁也要全民性地形成一种社会风尚，方可称之为成熟。否则，依然是“杯水车薪”之仁。孟子曾说“恻隐之心，仁之端也”，如何才能使“仁”得以成熟？人人都有的恻隐之心，如果不能得以充分显现，则称不上成熟。也就是说，仅仅依靠个人行为是难以完成的，需要的是大家共同努力。在这里，孟子对仁的复兴依然充满着期待与希望。

11.20

孟子曰："羿之教人射，必志于彀[1]；学者亦必志于彀。大匠诲人，必以规矩；学者亦必以规矩。"

Mencius said, "Yi, in teaching men to shoot, made it a rule to draw the bow to the full, and his pupils also did the same. A master workman, in teaching others, uses the compass and square, and his pupils do the same."

【注释】［1］志：期望。彀（gòu）：把弓拉满。

【译文】孟子说："羿教人射箭，一定要求把弓拉满；学射的人也力求自己把弓拉满。高明的工匠教人手艺，一定要用圆规和尺子；学手艺的人也一定要使用圆规和尺子。"

【解读】孟子在这里说“大匠诲人，必以规矩”，这是历史的定律。做事情应该遵循一定的方法和规矩，所谓没有规矩不成方圆。小到射箭，大到治国平天下，凡事都要有法可依，有规矩可循。既然凡事都需要一定的法度才可成就，那么老师舍弃了规矩则没法施教，学生失去了规矩则无法求学。学习射箭和木匠工艺尚且如此，学习圣人之道不就更是如此了吗？

告子下

Gaozi 2

12.1

任[1]人有问屋庐子[2]曰："礼与食孰重？"

曰："礼重。"

"色与礼孰重？"

曰："礼重。"

曰："以礼食，则饥而死；不以礼食，则得食，必以礼乎？亲迎[3]，则不得妻；不亲迎，则得妻，必亲迎乎？"

屋庐子不能对，明日之邹以告孟子。

孟子曰："于答是也何有？不揣其本而齐其末，方寸之木可使高于岑楼[4]。金重于羽者，岂谓一钩金[5]与一舆羽之谓哉？取食之重者，与礼之轻者而比之，奚翅[6]食重？取色之重者，与礼之轻者而比之，奚翅色重？往应之曰：'紾[7]兄之臂而夺之食，则得食；不紾，则不得食，则将紾之乎？逾东家墙而搂其处子[8]，则得妻；不搂，则不得妻，则将搂之乎？"

A man of Ren asked the disciple Wulu, saying, "Is an observance of the rules of propriety in regard to eating, or eating merely, the more important?"

The answer was, "The observance of the rules of propriety is the more important."

"Is the gratifying the appetite of sex, or the doing so only according to the rules of propriety, the more important?"

The answer again was, "The observance of the rules of propriety in the matter is the more important."

The man pursued, "If the result of eating only according to the rules of propriety will be death by starvation, while by disregarding those rules we may get food, must they still be observed in such a case? If according to the rule that he shall go in person to meet his wife a man cannot get married, while by disregarding that rule he may get married, must he still observe the rule in such a case?"

Wulu was unable to reply to these questions,

and the next day he went to Zou, and told them to Mencius.

Mencius said, "What difficulty is there in answering these inquiries? If you do not adjust them at their lower extremities, but only put their tops on a level, a piece of wood an inch square may be made to be higher than the pointed peak of a high building. Gold is heavier than feathers; — but does that saying have reference, on the one hand, to a single clasp of gold, and, on the other, to a waggon-load of feathers? If you take a case where the eating is of the utmost importance and the observing the rules of propriety is of little importance, and compare the things together, why stop with saying merely that the eating is more important? So, taking the case where the gratifying the appetite of sex is of the utmost importance and the observing the rules of propriety is of little importance, why stop with merely saying that the gratifying the appetite is the more important? Go and answer him thus, 'If, by twisting your elder brother's arm, and snatching from him what he is eating, you can get food for yourself, while, if you do not do so, you will not get anything to eat, will you so twist his arm? If by getting over your neighbour's wall, and dragging away his virgin daughter, you can get a wife, while if you do not do so, you will not be able to get a wife, will you so drag her away?' "

【注释】[1]任：春秋战国时的国家，故址在今山东济宁。[2]屋庐子：孟子的学生。[3]亲迎：古代婚礼环节，新郎亲迎新娘。这里代指按礼制娶亲。[4]岑楼：高楼。[5]一钩金：即一衣带钩那样一点点金。钩：衣带钩。[6]翅：同"啻"，只，止。[7]紾（zhěn）：扭转。[8]处子：处女。

【译文】有个任国人问屋庐子说："礼节与饮食哪样重要？"

孟子与屋庐子论“礼”　杨晓刚 绘

（屋庐子）说：“礼节重要。”

（那人又问：）“娶妻和礼节哪样重要？”

（屋庐子）说：“礼节重要。”

（那人又问：）“如果按照礼节来求食物，就只有饿死；不按照礼节来求食物，就可以得到食物，那还一定要按照礼节吗？如果按照亲迎礼节娶亲，就娶不到妻子；不按照亲迎礼节娶亲，就可以娶到妻子，那也一定要行亲迎礼吗？”

屋庐子不能回答，第二天到邹国把这个问题告诉了孟子。

孟子说：“回答这个问题有什么困难呢？不估量基础的高低，只比较它们的末端，那么方寸大小的树木可以使它高过高楼。金属比羽毛重，难道是说一个小金钩比一车羽毛还重吗？拿食物的重要方面与礼节的轻微方面相比较，何止是食物重要？拿娶妻的重要方面与礼的轻微方面相比较，何止是娶妻重要？回去这样应答说：‘扭住哥哥的胳膊抢夺他的食物，就可以得到吃的；不扭，便得不到吃的，那就该扭他吗？翻越东邻家的墙去搂抱人家的闺女，就可以得到妻子；不去搂抱，便得不到妻子，那就该去搂抱吗？”

【解读】礼是儒家哲学的重要概念，本章是孟子对礼的维护和捍卫，他既指出了礼的重要意义，又承认其意义具有相对性。任国人把礼与食、色相比较，也就是与生存和繁衍对立起来，如此一来就把这个问题推向了极致。孟子反驳的要点是抓住了此论用细小的礼节对比生存、繁衍之大节，不看根本而比较其末梢，故而以诡辩对诡辩、以极端对极端去反驳对方，表现出孟子高超的智慧和过人的辩才。生存和繁衍，是人类的大事，但这与儒家学说之尊礼并不对立。尊礼是为了“教以人伦：父子有亲，君臣有义，夫妇有别，长幼有序，朋友有信”，这便是人有别于禽兽的关键之所在。

12.2

曹交[1]问曰："人皆可以为尧、舜，有诸？"

孟子曰："然。"

"交闻文王十尺，汤九尺，今交九尺四寸以长，食粟而已，如何则可？"

曰："奚有于是？亦为之而已矣。有人于此，力不能胜一匹雏[2]，则为无力人矣；今曰举百钧，则为有力人矣。然则举乌获[3]之任，是亦为乌获而已矣。夫人岂以不胜为患哉？弗为耳。徐行后长者谓之弟，疾行先长者谓之不弟。夫徐行者，岂人所不能哉？所不为也。尧、舜之道，孝弟而已矣。子服尧之服，诵尧之言，行尧之行，是尧而已矣；子服桀之服，诵桀之言，行桀之行，是桀而已矣。"

曰："交得见于邹君，可以假馆[4]，愿留而受业于门。"

曰："夫道，若大路然，岂难知哉？人

病不求耳。子归而求之，有余师。”

Jiao of Cao asked Mencius, saying, “It is said, ‘All men may be Yaos and Shuns;’ —is it so?”

Mencius replied, “It is.”

Jiao went on, “l have heard that king Wen was ten cubits high, and Tang nine. Now I am nine cubits four inches in height. But I can do nothing but eat my millet. What am I to do to realize that saying?”

Mencius answered him, “What has this—the question of size— to do with the matter? It all lies simply in acting as such. Here is a man, whose strength was not equal to lift a duckling: —he was then a man of no strength. But today he says, ‘I can lift 3,000 catties’ weight,’ and he is a man of strength. And so, he who can lift the weight which Wu Huo lifted is just another Wu Huo. Why should a man make a want of ability the subject of his grief? It is only that he will not do the thing. To walk slowly, keeping behind his elders, is to perform the part of a younger brother. To walk quickly and precede his elders, is to violate the duty of a younger brother. Now, is it what a man cannot do—to walk slowly? It is what he does not do. The course of Yao and Shun was simply that of filial piety and fraternal duty. Wear the clothes of Yao, repeat the words of Yao, and do the actions of Yao, and you will just be a Yao. And, if you wear the clothes of Jie, repeat the words of Jie, and do the actions of Jie, you will just be a Jie.

Jiao said, "I shall be having an interview with the prince of Zou, and can ask him to let me have a house to lodge in. I wish to remain here, and receive instruction at your gate."

Mencius replied, "The way of truth is like a great road. It is not difficult to know it. The evil is only that men will not seek it. Do you go home and search for it, and you will have abundance of teachers."

【注释】［1］曹交：赵岐认为是曹君之弟，名交。［2］一匹雏：一只小鸡。［3］乌获：古代传说中的大力士。［4］假馆：借客舍，意为找一个住处。

【译文】曹交问道："人人都可以成为尧、舜，有这说法吗？"

孟子说："有。"

（曹交说：）"我听说周文王身高一丈，商汤身高九尺，如今我身高九尺四寸多，却只会吃饭罢了，要怎样做才行呢？"

（孟子）说："这有什么关系呢？只要去做就行了。要是有人，他的力气连一只小鸡都提不起来，那他便是一个没有力气的人；如果有人能够举起三千斤，那他就是一个大力士。同样的道理，举得起乌获所举的重量的，也就是乌获了。人难道以不能胜任为忧心吗？

只是不去做罢了。比如说，慢步走在长者之后叫作悌；快步抢在长者之前叫作不悌。那慢一点走难道是人做不到的吗？不去做罢了。尧舜之道，不过就是孝和悌而已。你穿尧的衣服，说尧的话，做尧的事，你便是尧了；你穿桀的衣服，说桀的话，做桀的事，你便是桀了。”

（曹交）说：“我准备去拜见邹君，向他借个住处，情愿留在您的门下做弟子。”

（孟子）说：“道就像大路一样，难道是难以了解吗？人们的问题只是不肯去探求罢了。你回去自己努力寻求吧，老师多得很呢。”

【解读】人皆可以为尧、舜，这是以孟子为代表的先秦儒家的重要论断，也符合“性善论”的哲学原理。尧、舜是天下共知的圣人，但尧、舜仅仅有两位，万千的人还是普通人，极个别人甚至是危害社会的恶人。基于此，曹交代表天下人发出了这一“大哉之问”。孟子立即做出了相当肯定的回答，并指出人成为圣贤不是不能，而是不为。

孟子的“性善论”就是肯定了人天生就有向善的本性，这种本性就潜伏在人的内心之中，只要加强修养，不被纷杂的外部事物所困扰，就能做到至诚至善，进而做到修身齐家治国平天下，就会达到尧、舜的圣人境界。但假如人的天性之善，在后天社会环境中受到利益的诱惑而任其私欲膨胀，必然会走向善的反面，走向不仁不义，不仅做不到尧、舜，反而容易成为夏桀式的暴君了。

12.3

公孙丑问曰："高子[1]曰：'《小弁》[2]，小人之诗也。'"

孟子曰："何以言之？"

曰："怨。"

曰："固[3]哉，高叟之为诗也！有人于此，越人关[4]弓而射之，则己谈笑而道之；无他，疏之也。其兄关弓而射之，则己垂涕泣而道之；无他，戚[5]之也。《小弁》之怨，亲亲也。亲亲，仁也。固矣夫，高叟之为诗也！"

曰："《凯风》[6]何以不怨？"

曰："《凯风》，亲之过小者也；《小弁》，亲之过大者也。亲之过大而不怨，是愈疏也；亲之过小而怨，是不可矶[7]也。愈疏，不孝也；不可矶，亦不孝也。孔子曰：'舜其至孝矣，五十而慕。'"

Gongsun Chou asked about an opinion of the

scholar Gao, saying, "Gao observed, 'The *Xiao Pan* is the ode of a little man.' "

Mencius asked, "Why did he say so?"

"Because of the murmuring which it expresses," was the reply.

Mencius answered, "How stupid was that old Gao in dealing with the ode! There is a man here, and a native of Yue bends his bow to shoot him. I will advise him not to do so, but speaking calmly and smilingly; —for no other reason but that he is not related to me. But if my own brother be bending his bow to shoot the man, then I will advise him not to do so, weeping and crying the while; —for no other reason than that he is related to me. The dissatisfaction expressed in the *Xiao Pan* is the working of relative affection, and that affection shows benevolence. Stupid indeed was old Gao's criticism on the ode."

Chou then said, "How is it that there is no

dissatisfaction expressed in the *Kai Feng*?"

Mencius replied, "The parentis fault referred to in the *Kai Feng* is small; that referred to in the *Xiao Pan* is great. Where the parent's fault was great, not to have murmured on account of it would have increased the want of natural affection. Where the parent's fault was small, to have murmured on account of it would have been to act like water which frets and foams about a stone that interrupts its course. To increase the want of natural affection would have been unfilial, and to fret and foam in such a manner would also have been unfilial. Confucius said, 'Shun was indeed perfectly filial! And yet, when he was fifty, he was full of longing desire about his parents.' "

【注释】［1］高子：齐人，年龄比孟子大，故孟子下文称其为“高叟”。［2］《小弁》：《诗经·小雅》中篇名。弁（pán），快乐。［3］固：

呆板。[4]关：通“弯”，拉满弓。[5]戚：亲。[6]《凯风》：《诗经·邶风》中篇名。[7]矶：这里作动词，水冲击岩石，引申为激怒，触犯。

【译文】公孙丑问道：“高子说：《小弁》是小人所作的诗。”

孟子说：“为什么这么说呢？”

（公孙丑）说：“诗中多有怨情。”

（孟子）说：“固执啊，高老先生这样解诗！如果有一个人在此，越国人弯弓去射他，他可以谈笑风生地讲这件事；没有别的原因，只因和越国人关系疏远。如果是他兄长弯弓射他，他就会痛哭流涕地讲这件事；没有其他原因，只因为和兄长的关系亲近。《小弁》中的怨恨，是亲近亲人。亲近亲人，就是仁。真是固执啊，高老先生这样解诗！”

（公孙丑）问：“《凯风》这首诗为什么没有忧怨呢？”

（孟子）说：“《凯风》这首诗，是因为至亲的过错较小；《小弁》，是因为至亲的过错较大。至亲的过错较大而不怨恨，是更加疏远父母；至亲过错较小而怨恨，这是自己承受不了一点刺激。更加疏远父母，这是不孝；自己不能受一点刺激，也是不孝。孔子说过：‘舜是最孝顺的了，到了五十岁还眷念着父母。’”

【解读】本章通过解诗而论述孝道。高子可能是当时的解诗名家，孟子毫不客气地指出高子解读《小弁》未免死板和狭隘，没有从诗韵之中体味到孝道的真谛，这体现了孟子对孝道的深刻认识。

传说，周幽王废立了太子宜臼，《小弁》这首诗就是太子宜臼或他的老师所作。孟子从“亲之过大”而产生的怨恨中看到的是“亲亲”，是“仁”的表现，理解到作者是对其父周幽王不合“礼”的无奈，是出于对父王的孝。孟子运用“知人论世”的方法，同样回答了《凯风》一诗中“亲之过小”而产生的不怨，其实也是对父母的一种孝。他在此基础上进一步指出，“亲之过大”，当“怨”，否则就是漠不关心的“愈疏”表现，这是不孝。“亲之过小”，当不怨，否则就是过于敏感的“不可矶”表现，也是不孝。孟子在这里对孝的判断，体现出儒家的中庸思想。后世的所谓“孝顺”，重“顺”而轻孝，走上极端。

孟子借解诗论述的孝道，于今天社会仍然有重要的借鉴意义。真正的孝，不是不指出父母的不足，有时候指出缺点和不足恰恰说明对父母的爱。比如，有的老年人沉浸在虚假保健品的宣传中不能自拔，这时候真正孝顺的儿女，当“怨”则怨；同时，也能容忍父母的小毛病、小过失。比如父母都爱唠叨，这时候真正孝顺的儿女，就应当倾听。

12.4

宋牼[1]将之楚，孟子遇于石丘[2]，曰："先生将何之？"

曰："吾闻秦、楚构兵[3]，我将见楚王说[4]而罢之。楚王不悦，我将见秦王说而罢之。二王我将有所遇[5]焉。"

曰："轲也请无问其详，愿闻其指。说之将何如？"

曰："我将言其不利也。"

曰："先生之志则大矣，先生之号[6]则不可。先生以利说秦、楚之王，秦、楚之王悦于利，以罢三军之师，是三军之士乐罢而悦于利也。为人臣者怀利以事其君，为人子者怀利以事其父，为人弟者怀利以事其兄。是君臣、父子、兄弟终去仁义，怀利以相接，然而不亡者，未之有也。先生以仁义说秦、楚之王，秦、楚之王悦于仁义，而罢三军之师，是三军之士乐罢而悦于仁义也。为人臣者怀仁义以事其君，为人子者怀仁义以事其父，为人弟者怀仁义以事其兄，是君臣、父子、兄弟去利，怀仁义以相接也。然而不王者，未之有也。何必曰利？”

Song Keng being about to go to Chu, Mencius met him in Shiqiu. “Master, where are you going?” asked Mencius.

Keng replied, “I have heard that Qin and Chu are fighting together, and I am going to see the king of Chu and persuade him to cease hostilities. If he shall not be pleased with my advice, I shall go to see the king of Qin, and persuade him in the same way. Of the two kings I shall surely find that I can succeed with one of them.”

Mencius said, “I will not venture to ask about the particulars, but I should like to hear the scope of your plan. What course will you take to try to persuade them?”

Keng answered, "I will tell them how unprofitable their course is to them."

"Master," said Mencius, "your aim is great, but your argument is not good. If you, starting from the point of profit, offer your persuasive counsels to the kings of Qin and Chu, and if those kings are pleased with the consideration of profit so as to stop the movements of their armies, then all belonging to those armies will rejoice in the cessation of war, and find their pleasure in the pursuit of profit. Ministers will serve their sovereign for the profit of which they cherish the thought; sons will serve their fathers, and younger brothers will serve their elder brothers, from the same consideration—and the issue will be, that, abandoning benevolence and righteousness, sovereign and minister, father and son, younger brother and elder, will carry on all their intercourse with this thought of profit cherished in their breasts. But never has there been such a state of society, without ruin being the result of it. If you, starting from the ground of benevolence and righteousness, offer your counsels to the kings of Qin and Chu, and if those kings are pleased with the consideration of benevolence and righteousness so as to stop the operations of their armies, then all belonging to those armies will rejoice in the stopping from war, and find their pleasure in benevolence and righteousness. Ministers will serve their sovereign, cherishing the principles of benevolence and righteousness; sons will serve their fathers, and younger brothers will serve their elder brothers, in the same way—and so, sovereign and minister, father and son, elder brother and younger, abandoning the thought of profit, will cherish the principles of benevolence and righteousness, and carry on all their intercourse upon them. But never has there been such a state of society, without the state where it prevailed rising to the royal sway. Why must you use that word 'profit?' "

【注释】［1］宋轻（kēng）：宋国人，又名宋钘，战国时期著名思想家。［2］石丘：地名，所在不详。［3］构兵：交战。［4］说（shuì）：劝说。［5］遇：说合。［6］号：号辞，辞令，交际场合应对得宜的话语。

【译文】宋轻正在准备去楚国，孟子在石丘遇上了他，问道："先生准备上哪里去？"

（宋轻）说："我听说秦国和楚国在交战，我想去见楚王，劝说他停战。如果楚王不高兴听，我再去见秦王，劝说他停战。两位君王中我总能劝说通一个吧。"

（孟子）说："我不想问得太详细，只想了解你的主要想法。你打算怎样去劝说他们呢？"

（宋轻）说："我打算指出交战的不利之处。"

（孟子）说："先生的动机是远大的，但先生这种言辞却不行。先生用利去劝说秦王、楚王，秦王、楚王喜欢对自己有利而让军队休战，这样也就使军队官兵感到有利于自己才乐于停战。做臣子的怀着求利的念头侍奉国君，做儿子的怀着求利的念头侍奉父亲，做弟弟的怀着求利的念头侍奉哥哥，这会使君臣、父子、兄弟终将背离仁义，怀着求利的念头相互对待，这样的国家却不灭亡，是从来没有过的。如果先生用仁义去劝说秦王、楚王，秦王、楚王喜爱仁义而让军队休战，这就会使军队因为喜爱仁义而乐于停战。做臣子的心怀仁义侍奉国君，做儿子的心怀仁义侍奉父亲，做弟弟的心怀仁义侍奉哥哥，这样就会使君臣、父子、兄弟去掉求利的念头，而怀着仁义之心相互对待了。这样还不能使天下归服的，是从来没有的。何必要说利呢？”

【解读】义利之辨是理解孟子思想的重要切入口。《孟子》一书，开篇即辨义利，孟子对义利的基本立场是一贯的、毫不动摇的。仁义优先，仁义至上，这是治国理政、推行王道的最基本原则。孟子从仁义的角度来阐述停止战争达到和平，尽管有着非常强烈的理想主义色彩，但却是思想家引领整个社会正能量之所必需。从利益出发，人们考虑的只是自己的私利，那么君臣、父子、兄弟就有可能因为利益冲突而背信弃义，反目成仇，成为“大害”；从仁义出发，人们考虑的是以德服人，仁义充满大爱，如此君臣、父子、兄弟就会上下一心，成为“大利”。所以，孟子看问题，都是直指问题的本质，达到实施仁政的目的。在群雄逐利的战国时代，孟子的这一理想看似很“迂阔”而不合时宜，但从大历史的角度审视，天下一统，王道推行，确需凭借仁义的实施。

12.5

孟子居邹，季任[1]为任处守，以币交，受之而不报[2]。处于平陆[3]，储子[4]为相，以币交，受之而不报。他日由邹之任，见季子；由平陆之齐，不见储子。屋庐子喜曰："连得间[5]矣。"问曰："夫子之任见季子；之齐不见储子，为其为相与？"

曰："非也。《书》曰：'享[6]多仪，仪不及物曰不享，惟不役[7]志于享。'为其不成享也。"

屋庐子悦。或问之。屋庐子曰："季子不得之邹，储子得之平陆。"

When Mencius was residing in Zou, the younger brother of the chief of Ren, who was guardian of Ren at the time, paid his respects to him by a present of silks, which Mencius received, not going to acknowledge it. When he was sojourning in Pinglu, Chu, who was prime minister of the state, sent him a similar present, which he received in the same way. Subsequently, going from Zou to Ren, he visited the guardian; but when he went from Ping-lu to the capital of Qi, he did not visit the minister Chu. The disciple Wulu was glad, and said, "I have got an opportunity to obtain some instruction." He asked accordingly, "Master, when you went to Ren, you visited the chief's brother; and when you went to Qi, you did not visit Chu. Was it not because he is only the minister?"

Mencius replied, "No. It is said in the *Book of History,* 'In presenting an offering to a superior, most depends on the demonstrations of respect. If those demonstrations are not equal to the things offered, we say there is no offering, that is, there is no act of the will presenting the offering.' This is because the things so offered do not constitute an offering to a superior."

Wulu was pleased, and when some one asked him what Mencius meant, he said, "The younger of Ren could not go to Zou, but the minister Chu might have gone to Pinglu."

【注释】［1］季任：任国国君的弟弟。［2］报：回谢。［3］平陆：地名，齐国的下邑，故城在今山东汶上。［4］储子：齐国人，曾与孟子交。［5］连：屋庐子之名。得间：发现差错。［6］享：享献之礼。［7］役：用。

【译文】孟子居住在邹国的时候，季任正在任国代理国政，送礼物来结交孟子，孟子收了礼物却不回谢。孟子居住在平陆的时候，储子担任齐国的相，送礼物来结交孟子，孟子收了礼也不回谢。后来，孟子从邹国到了任国，拜访了季子；从平陆到了齐国，却不拜访储子。屋庐子高兴地说："我发现老师的差错了。"问道："老师到了任国，拜访了季子；到了齐国，不拜访储子，是因为储子只是担任国相吗？”

（孟子）说：“不是的。《尚书》上说：‘进献礼品看重礼仪，礼仪配不上礼品，就叫没有进献，因为心意不在进献上。’这是因为他没有完成进献的缘故。”

屋庐子听了很高兴。有人问他这件事，屋庐子说：“季子（代理任国国政）不能随意到邹国去，而储子（作为国相）是能亲自到平陆去的，他为什么只送礼而不自己去呢。”

【解读】孟子同样是接受礼物，而是否回拜却截然不同，耐人寻味。孟子是“礼”的坚定捍卫者与执行者，他认为礼物无论轻重，不但看其心意是否真诚，更重要的是还要看其行为是否合乎礼仪。依礼制，代理国政期间是不能擅自离职的，故而季子不能亲自把礼物送给孟子，所以孟子收到礼物后，俟机依礼回拜了季子；而孟子到了齐国之所以没有回拜储子，是因为储子担任齐国的相，是可以亲自来平陆送礼，所以孟子认为储子没有或者说缺乏诚意。虽然季子代理国政比储子担任国相的官职大，但这并不是孟子有选择性回拜的原因，在孟子道德的天平里，不以官职论尊卑，只有“礼”是最高标准。

12.6

淳于髡[1]曰："先名实[2]者，为人也；后名实者，自为也。夫子[3]在三卿之中，名实未加于上下而去之，仁者固如此乎？"

孟子曰："居下位，不以贤事不肖者，伯夷也；五就汤，五就桀者，伊尹也；不恶污君，不辞小官者，柳下惠也。三子者不同道，其趋[4]一也。一者何也？曰：仁也。君子亦仁而已矣，何必同？"

曰："鲁缪公[5]之时，公仪子[6]为政，子柳、子思为臣，鲁之削也滋甚。若是乎，贤者之无益于国也！"

曰："虞不用百里奚而亡，秦穆公用之而霸。不用贤则亡，削何可得与？"

曰："昔者王豹处于淇[7]，而河西善讴；绵驹[8]处于高唐，而齐右[9]善歌；华周、杞梁之妻善哭其夫[10]，而变国俗。有诸内必形诸外。为其事而无其功者，髡未尝睹之也。

是故无贤者也，有则髡必识之。”

曰：“孔子为鲁司寇，不用，从而祭，燔肉不至，不税冕[11]而行。不知者以为为肉也，其知者以为为无礼也。乃孔子则欲以微罪行，不欲为苟去。君子之所为，众人固不识也。”

Chunyu Kun said, “He who makes fame and meritorious services his first objects, acts with a regard to others. He who makes them only secondary objects, acts with a regard to himself. You, master, were ranked among the three chief ministers of the state, but before your fame and services had reached either to the prince or the people, you have left your place. Is this indeed the way of the benevolent?”

Mencius replied, “There was Boyi; —he abode in an inferior situation, and would not, with his virtue, serve a degenerate prince. There was Yi Yin; —he five times went to Tang, and five times went to Jie. There was Hui of Liuxia; —he did not disdain to serve a vile prince, nor did he decline a small office. The courses pursued by those three worthies were different, but their aim was one. And what was their one aim? We must answer —'To be perfectly virtuous.' And so it is simply after this that superior men strive. Why must they all pursue the same course?"

Kun pursued, "In the time of the duke Mu of Lu, the government was in the hands of Gongyi, while Ziliu and Zisi were ministers. And yet, the dismemberment of Lu then increased exceedingly. Such was the case, a specimen how your men of virtue are of no advantage to a kingdom!"

Mencius said, "The prince of Yu did not use Baili Xi, and thereby lost his state. The duke Mu of Qin used him, and became chief of all the princes. Ruin is the consequence of not employing men of virtue and talents; —how can it rest with dismemberment merely?"

Kun urged again, "Formerly, when Wang Bao dwelt on the Qi, the people on the west of the Yellow River all became skilful at singing in his abrupt manner. When Mian Ju lived in Gaotang, the people in the parts of Qi on the west became skilful at singing in his prolonged manner. The wives of Hua Zhou and Qi Liang bewailed their husbands so skilfully, that they changed the manners of the state. When there is the gift within, it manifests itself without. I have never seen the man who could do the deeds of a worthy, and did not realize the work of one. Therefore there are now no men of talents and virtue. If there were, I should know them."

Mencius answered, "When Confucius was chief minister of justice in Lu, the prince came not to follow his counsels. Soon after there was the solstitial sacrifice, and when a part of the flesh presented in sacrifice was not sent to him, he went away even without taking off his cap of ceremony. Those who

did not know him supposed it was on account of the flesh. Those who knew him supposed that it was on account of the neglect of the usual ceremony. The fact was, that Confucius wanted to go away on occasion of some small offence, not wishing to do so without some apparent cause. All men cannot be expected to understand the conduct of a superior man."

【注释】［1］淳于髡（kūn）：战国时期齐国著名的政治家和思想家，以博学多才、善于辩论著称，是稷下学宫中的著名学者之一。［2］名：声誉。实：事功。［3］夫子：指孟子。［4］趋：趋向，目标。［5］鲁缪公：即鲁穆公。［6］公仪子：即公仪休。曾经当过鲁相，奉法循礼治理鲁国。［7］王豹：卫国人，善歌者。淇：淇水，古黄河支流。［8］绵驹：齐国人，善歌者。［9］齐右：高唐位于齐国西部，古人以西方为右。［10］华周、杞梁之妻善哭：华周、杞梁均为齐国勇士，战死后其妻向城而哭，以致城墙一角坍塌，影响到一国民俗都善哭。孟姜女的故事即由此衍化而来。[11]税(tuō)：同“脱”。冕：祭祀时所戴的礼冠。

【译文】淳于髡说：“首先重视名望功业的，是为了天下的人；而后重视名望功业的，是为了独善其身。先生您位列齐国三卿，名望功业还没有贡献于上（齐王）下（百姓）就辞职而去了，仁人本就该这样的吗？”

孟子说：“处在低下的地位，不以贤能侍奉不成器的人，这是伯夷；五次到汤那里做事，五次到桀那里做事，这是伊尹；不讨厌昏庸的君主，不拒绝微小的官职，这是柳下惠。三个人的人生道路不同，但目标是一致的。一致的目标是什么呢？就是“仁”啊。君子只要做到“仁”就行，何必要处处相同？”

（淳于髡）说：“鲁缪公的时候，公仪子掌管政事，子柳、子思也在朝做臣，然而鲁国国力被削弱的很严重。如此看来，贤者对于国家没有增益啊！”

（孟子）说：“虞国因为不任用百里奚而亡国，秦穆公用了他就称霸了。可见不用贤人就会亡国，何止是国力削弱呢？”

（淳于髡）说：“从前王豹居住在淇水边上，河西的人因此而善于唱歌；绵驹居住在高唐，齐国西部的人因此而善于唱歌；华周、杞梁的妻子，为丈夫的死而哭得异常伤心，因而改变了一国的风气。内部有什么，一定会表现在外部。做了一件事而不见这件事的功效，我还没有见过这种情况呢。所以现在是没有贤人，要有，我一定会知道的。”

（孟子）说：“孔子担任鲁国的司寇，不受信任，有一次跟随（鲁国国君）去祭祀，祭肉不按规定送来，于是顾不上脱掉祭祀时所戴的礼帽就走了。不了解孔子的，以为他是为了那点祭肉而离开的，了解孔子的，认为他是因为鲁君的失礼而离开的。而孔子却正想担点儿小罪名离开，不想随便弃官而去。君子所做的事，一般人本就是不理解的。”

【解读】本章三问三答，记录了一段历史，也反映出孟子的内心世界。齐国著名辩士淳于髡想挽留孟子，而孟子却去意已定。

首先，淳于髡抛出读书人的一个重要命题：立业扬名，拯救世人，将名誉与功业看得至为重要；或者独善其身，隐居江湖，将名誉与功业看得无足轻重。孟子身居上卿，功名未立就辞职而去，这是仁德之人所为吗？淳于髡抓住了孟子积极入世推行仁政的终极目的，可谓切中要害。然而孟子举出伯夷、伊尹、柳下惠三人事例，说明一个人所处社会环境不同，进退、行为自然不同，但这些古代圣贤求仁的心志、目标是一致的。所以名誉与功业都要以推行仁政为准则，既然推行不了，名誉与功业又有什么重要的呢？

淳于髡见“名实”没有诱惑力，又举出

贤德之人对国家无用的事例，孟子以其人之道，反治其人之身，说明没有贤德之人可以亡国，有了贤德之人可以兴国。

最后，淳于髡以激将法发起更强的诘问：贤德之人，一定要有行动，有行动才会有改变，王豹、绵驹及二位善哭夫人就改变了齐国的风俗。言外之意，你孟子在齐国，对齐国没有什么实际贡献，由此看出你孟子根本不是贤德之人。孟子没有直接回答，而是举出孔子离开鲁国的事例，说明贤德之人的所作所为，一般人根本不理解，甚至还会曲解。

12.7

孟子曰："五霸者，三王之罪人也；今之诸侯，五霸之罪人也；今之大夫，今之诸侯之罪人也。天子适诸侯曰巡狩，诸侯朝于天子曰述职。春省[1]耕而补不足，秋省敛而助不给。入其疆，土地辟，田野治，养老尊贤，俊杰在位，则有庆[2]，庆以地。入其疆，土地荒芜，遗老失贤，掊克[3]在位，则有让[4]。一不朝，则贬其爵；再不朝，则削其地；三不朝，则六师移之。是故天子讨而不伐，诸侯伐而不讨。五霸者，搂诸侯以伐诸侯者也，故曰：五霸者，三王之罪人也。五霸，桓公为盛。葵丘之会[5]诸侯，束牲、载书而不歃血[6]。初命曰：'诛不孝，无易树子，无以妾为妻。'再命曰：'尊贤育才，以彰有德。'三命曰：'敬老慈幼，无忘宾旅。'四命曰：'士无世官，官事无摄，取士必得，无专杀大夫。'五命曰：'无曲防，无遏籴，无有封而不告。'曰：'凡我同盟之人，既盟之后，言归于好。’今之诸侯皆犯此五禁，故曰：今之诸侯，五霸之罪人也。长君之恶其罪小，逢君之恶其罪大。今之大夫，皆逢君之恶，故曰：今之大夫，今之诸侯之罪人也。”

Mencius said, “The five chiefs of the princes were sinners against the three kings. The princes of the present day are sinners against the five chiefs. The great officers of the present day are sinners against the princes. The sovereign visited the princes, which was called ‘A tour of inspection.’ The princes attended at the court of the sovereign, which was called ‘Giving a report of office.’ It was a custom in the spring to examine the ploughing, and supply any deficiency of seed; and in autumn to examine the reaping, and assist where there was a deficiency of the crop. When the sovereign entered the boundaries of a state, if the new ground was being reclaimed, and the old fields well cultivated; if the old were nourished and the worthy honoured; and if men of distinguished talents were placed in office: then the prince was rewarded,— rewarded with an addition to his territory. On the other hand, if, on entering a state, the ground was found left wild or overrun with weeds; if the old were neglected and the worthy unhonoured; and if the offices were filled with hard tax-gatherers: then the prince was reprimanded. If a prince once omitted his attendance at court, he was punished by degradation of rank; if he did so a second time, he was deprived of a portion of his territory; if he did so a third time, the royal forces were set in motion, and he was removed from his government. Thus the sovereign commanded the punishment, but did not himself inflict it, while the princes inflicted the punishment, but did not command it. The five chiefs, however, dragged the princes to punish other princes, and hence I say that they were sinners against the three kings.

"Of the five chiefs the most powerful was the duke Huan. At the assembly of the princes in Kuiqiu, he bound the victim and placed the writing upon it, but did not slay it to smear their mouths with the blood. The first injunction in their agreement was, 'Slay the unfilial; change not the son who has been appointed heir; exalt not a concubine to be the wife.' The second was, 'Honour the worthy, and maintain the talented, to give distinction to the virtuous.' The third was, 'Respect the old, and be kind to the young. Be not forgetful of strangers and travellers.' The fourth was, 'Let not offices be hereditary, nor let officers be pluralists. In the selection of officers let the object be to get the proper men. Let not a ruler take it on himself to put to death a great officer.' The fifth was, 'Follow no crooked policy in making embankments. Impose no restrictions on the sale of grain. Let there be no promotions without first announcing them to the sovereign.' It was then said, 'All we who have united in this agreement shall hereafter maintain amicable relations.' The princes of the present day all violate these five prohibitions, and therefore I say that the princes of the present day are sinners against the five chiefs. The crime of him who connives at, and aids, the wickedness of his prince is small, but the crime of him who anticipates and excites that wickedness is great. The officers of the present day all go to meet their sovereigns' wickedness, and therefore I say that the great officers of the present day are sinners against the princes."

【注释】［1］省：巡察。［2］庆：奖赏。［3］掊（póu）克：聚敛，这里指聚敛民财的为政者。克：通“尅”。［4］让：责罚。［5］葵丘之会：葵丘之会发生于公元前651年，齐桓公在葵丘大会诸侯进而奠定了霸主地位，其事见载

于《左传·僖公九年》。［6］歃（shà）血：结盟时的一种仪式。立盟时杀牲取血，盟誓者口含其血，或涂于口旁，表示诚信。

【译文】孟子说："五霸，是三王的罪人；现在的诸侯，是五霸的罪人；现在的大夫，是现在诸侯的罪人。天子到诸侯那里去叫作巡狩，诸侯朝见天子叫作述职。天子春天视察耕种情况，是为了补助不足的农户；秋天视察收获情况，是为了救济缺粮农户。进入某个诸侯国，如果那里土地开垦得多，田野整治得好，老人得到赡养，贤人受到尊敬，有才能的人在位做官，那就有奖赏，拿土地作为奖赏。进入某个诸侯国，如果那里土地荒芜，遗弃老人，排斥贤人，贪官污吏在位，那就给予责罚。诸侯一次不朝见天子，就降他的爵位；两次不朝见，就削减他的封地；三次不朝见，就派军队去征讨他。所以天子发布命令声讨他的罪行，而不亲自征伐；诸侯负责征伐而不能声讨。五霸却是胁迫诸侯去讨伐别的诸侯，所以说五霸是三王的罪人。五霸中，齐桓公最强。在葵丘盟会上，诸侯们捆绑了牺牲，把盟书放在它身上，并不歃血。盟书第一条说：‘责罚不孝的人，不得擅自改立世子，不得把妾立为正妻。’第二条说：‘尊重贤人，培育人才，用来表彰有德行的人。’第三条说：‘要敬老爱幼，不要怠慢了来宾和旅客。’第四条说：‘士人不能世代做官，公职不能兼任，选用士人一定要得当，不得擅自杀戮大夫。’第五条说：‘不得到处修筑堤防，不得阻止邻国来买粮食，不能私自封赏而不报告盟主。’盟书最后说：‘凡是我们同盟的人，盟会之后都恢复友好关系。’现在的诸侯都违背了这五条誓约，所以说：现在的诸侯是五霸的罪人。助长了君王的过错，这个罪行还算小的；逢迎君王的过错，这个罪行就大了。现在的大夫都逢迎君王的过错，所以说：现在的大夫是现在诸侯的罪人。”

【解读】本章是声讨战国纷乱争斗局面的檄文，集中表现了孟子追随三王、实行仁政的治国理想。五霸，一般指春秋时期的齐桓公、晋文公、秦穆公、楚庄王、宋襄公。三王，即为夏商周三代立国之王，具体指禹、汤、文王或武王。

在孟子看来，以三王为代表的先代圣贤是最有盛德的，他们的道统之法，是治世安邦的典范；而春秋时期的五霸，虽然有治世之功，但他们没有遵循诸侯的职责，崇尚武力，相互征伐，实施的是“霸道”政治，背离了三王道统，因此是三王的罪人；到了孟子所在的战国时期，诸侯们既不知三王之法，又不讲道义甚至助纣为虐，故而战争频繁，民不聊生，因此他们是五霸的罪人；而诸侯们手下的官员比诸侯更差，一味讨好，曲意逢迎，因此他们是诸侯的罪人。孟子之所以如此说，理由是：天子履行了天子的职责，他们定期巡视、考察政绩、体察民情、奖罚分明。诸侯就应该履行好诸侯的职责吧，可社会现实则不然。

孟子以齐国为例，列举了“葵丘之会”，虽大义凛然地在盟书上写下“五禁”，但最终“今之诸侯皆犯此五禁”。而大夫理应辅助诸侯尊礼守道、避恶扬善，但“长君之恶”甚至“逢君之恶”成为一时现象。面对如此不堪现象，孟子怎能不愤然？春秋战国无义战，道德崩溃，社会失序，利益成为唯一的主导。

孟子一向富有强烈的现实关怀和批判精神，虽然生不逢时，没有真正实现仁政的治国理想，但勇于担当起儒家道统传承的责任与使命，进而担当起中华文化传承的道统和使命，为后代留下一代圣贤的伟岸形象。

12.8

鲁欲使慎子[1]为将军。孟子曰："不教民而用之，谓之殃民。殃民者，不容于尧、舜之世。一战胜齐，遂有南阳[2]，然且不可。"

慎子勃然不悦曰："此则滑厘所不识也。"

曰："吾明告子。天子之地方千里；不千里，不足以待诸侯。诸侯之地方百里；不百里，不足以守宗庙之典籍[3]。周公之封于鲁，为方百里也；地非不足，而俭于百里。太公之封于齐也，亦为方百里也；地非不足也，而俭于百里。今鲁方百里者五，子以为有王者作，则鲁在所损乎？在所益乎？徒取诸彼以与此，然且仁者不为，况于杀人以求之乎？君子之事君也，务引其君以当道，志于仁而已。"

The prince of Lu wanted to make the minister Shen commander of his army. Mencius said, "To employ an uninstructed people in war may be said to be destroying the people. A destroyer of the people would not have been tolerated in the times of Yao and Shun. Though by a single battle you should subdue Qi, and get possession of Nanyang, the thing ought not to be done."

Shen changed countenance, and said in displeasure, "This is what I, Guli, do not understand."

Mencius said, "I will lay the case plainly before you. The territory appropriated to the sovereign is 1,000 *li* square. Without a thousand *li*, he would not have sufficient for his entertainment of the princes. The territory appropriated to a Hou is 100 *li* square. Without 100 *li*, he would not have sufficient wherewith to observe the statutes kept in his ancestral temple. When Zhougong was invested with the principality of Lu, it was a hundred *li* square. The territory was indeed enough, but it was not more than 100 *li*. When Taigong was invested with the principality of Qi, it was 100 *li* square. The territory was indeed enough, but it was not more than 100 *li*. Now Lu is five times 100 *li* square. If a true royal ruler were to arise, whether do you think that Lu would be diminished or increased by him? If it were merely taking the place from the one state to give it to the other, a benevolent man would not do it; how much less will he do so, when the end is to be sought by the slaughter of men! The way in which a superior man serves his prince contemplates simply the leading him in the right path, and directing his mind to benevolence."

【注释】［1］慎子：名滑厘，善于用兵。［2］南阳：地名，在泰山西南、汶河以北，本属于鲁，后被齐侵夺。［3］典籍：这里指记载先祖典章法度的文册。

【译文】鲁国想让慎子担任将军。孟子说："不教化百姓就使用他们，这叫祸害百姓。祸害百姓的人，在尧舜时代是不容许存身的。一仗就打败了齐国，收回了南阳，然而还是不可以的。”

慎子很不高兴地说：“这话我滑厘听不明白了。”

（孟子）说：“我来明白地告诉你。天子的土地纵横千里；不到一千里，就不够接待诸侯前来朝觐。诸侯的土地纵横百里；不足一百里，就不够奉守宗庙里的礼制。当年周公分封在鲁地，是方圆百里；当时土地不是不够，只不过是俭约百里。当年姜太公分封在齐地，也是方圆百里；不是土地不够，只不过是俭约百里。现在鲁国的土地有方圆百里的五倍了，你认为有圣王出现，使得鲁国的土地应该削减呢？还是应该增加呢？白白把那里的土地取来并入这里，这样的事仁人尚且不做，何况用杀人的方式来求取土地呢？君子侍奉君主，只当一心一意地引导君主走正道，立志追求仁德就好了。”

【解读】本章强调治理国家不是以领土多少为重，而是以符合仁义道德原则为重。鲁国启用慎子，目的在于强军，保证领土安全，进而兼并更多的土地。这也是当时各诸侯国的共同表现。

孟子从爱护百姓生命出发，强调这种相互掠夺的战争，即使一战全胜也是不义之战。慎子正在兴头上，却被孟子泼了一头冷水，很不高兴。于是乎孟子从先贤封地说起，周公、姜太公的分封土地，之所以方圆百里，并不是土地不够分，而是制约他们的权势，刚好够礼法的标准即可。当初他们不谋求更多的封地，也就是不谋求更大的利益。但随着周王朝的衰败，群雄并起，逐鹿中原，孟子为之叹息。孟子提出："徒取诸彼以与此，然且仁者不为，况于杀人以求之乎？"言下之意就是，富民强国并没有错，一统天下也并非不可以，但通过战争掠夺获得土地就不是仁者的作为了，做大做强要依靠"仁义礼智”道德的力量。只有为政者讲仁义，才具有广泛的影响力和号召力，百姓才会信服你、依附你。如此一来，有了人民的依附，土地自然归你所有，所以说“仁义”是解决土地问题的根本。

12.9

孟子曰："今之事君者皆曰：'我能为君辟土地，充府库。'今之所谓良臣，古之所谓民贼也。君不乡道[1]，不志于仁，而求富之，是富桀也。'我能为君约与国[2]，战必克。'今之所谓良臣，古之所谓民贼也。君不乡道，不志于仁，而求为之强战，是辅桀也。由今之道，无变今之俗，虽与之天下，不能一朝居也。"

Mencius said, "Those who nowadays serve their sovereigns say, 'We can for our sovereign enlarge the limits of the cultivated ground, and fill his treasuries and arsenals.' Such persons are nowadays called 'good ministers,' but anciently they were called 'robbers of the people.' If a sovereign follows not the right way, nor has his mind bent on benevolence, to seek to enrich him is to enrich a Jie.

Or they will say, 'We can for our sovereign form alliances with other states, so that our battles must be successful.' Such persons are nowadays called 'good ministers', but anciently they were called 'robbers of the people'. If a sovereign follows not the right way, nor has his mind directed to benevolence, to seek to enrich him is to enrich a Jie. Although a prince, pursuing the path of the present day, and not changing its practices, were to have the throne given to him, he could not retain it for a single morning."

【注释】［1］乡道：向往道德。乡：同"向"，向往。［2］与国：盟国。

【译文】孟子说："如今服侍国君的人都说：'我能为您开拓土地，充实府库。'如今所谓的良臣，就是古代所说的民贼。国君不向往道德，不立志行仁，为臣却想办法让他富有，这等于是去让夏桀富有。'我能够替国君邀约盟国，每战必胜。’如今所谓的良臣，就是古代所说的民贼。国君不向往道德，不立志行仁，为臣却去想法让他武力强大，这等于是去辅助夏桀。如今沿着这样的道路走下去，不改变现今的风俗习气，即便把整个天下给他，他也是一天都坐不稳的。”

【解读】本章紧承上章，进一步讲明孟子反对慎子、主张仁义的缘由。孟子态度极为鲜明地批判了那些不引导他的国君“志于仁”的“民贼”行为，是“富桀”和“辅桀”。国君不向道，不志于仁的追求，作为大臣依然为其开辟土地，充实国库，发动战争，就是在助纣为虐，就是在把百姓和国家都推向灾难的深渊。这样的臣子不是良臣，反而应该是民贼，是残害百姓的人。

判断是良臣还是民贼，就是看他是否辅助国君实施仁政，一切取决于“仁”。这些臣子可能是能臣，他们的计谋可能会取得“国富兵强”的显著成就，但不义的“霸道”与孟子的仁政“王道”针锋相对。所以他预言：“不志于仁”的国君即使有一天把天下都交给他，他是一天也坐不安稳的。后来的历史也一再证明孟子的先见之明，秦国的强大可谓不可一世，靠武力实现国家的大一统，但二世而亡，强大转化为虚无，就是明证。

12.10

白圭[1]曰："吾欲二十而取一，何如？"

孟子曰："子之道，貉[2]道也。万室之国，一人陶，则可乎？"

曰："不可，器不足用也。"

曰："夫貉，五谷不生，惟黍生之。无城郭、宫室、宗庙、祭祀之礼，无诸侯币帛饔飧[3]，无百官有司，故二十取一而足也。今居中国，去人伦，无君子[4]，如之何其可也？陶以寡，且不可以为国，况无君子乎？欲轻之于尧、舜之道者，大貉小貉也；欲重之于尧、舜之道者，大桀小桀也。"

Bai Gui said, "I want to take a twentieth of the produce only as the tax. What do you think of it?"

Mencius said, "Your way would be that of the Mo. In a country of ten thousand families, would it do to have only one potter?"

Gui replied, "No. The vessels would not be enough to use."

Mencius went on, "In Mo all the five kinds of grain are not grown; it only produces the millet. There are no fortified cities, no edifices, no ancestral temples, no ceremonies of sacrifice; there are no princes requiring presents and entertainments; there is no system of officers with their various subordinates. On these accounts a tax of one-twentieth of the produce is sufficient there. But now it is the Middle Kingdom that we live in. To banish the relationships of men, and have no superior men; —how can such a state of things be thought of? With but few potters a kingdom cannot subsist; —how much less can it subsist without men of a higher rank than others? If we wish to make the taxation lighter than the system of Yao and Shun, we shall just have a great Mo and a small Mo. If we wish to make it heavier, we shall just have the great Jie and the small Jie."

【注释】［1］白圭：名丹，字圭，曾任魏相，以筑堤治水而闻名。［2］貉（mò）：同“貊”，东北方的一个小国名。［3］饔飧（yōng sūn）：宴饮。［4］无君子：这里意指“无百官有司”的官吏。

【译文】白圭说：“我想采用二十抽一的税率，怎么样？”

孟子说：“您的做法，就是貉国的做法。有万户的国家，只有一个人制作陶器，可以吗？”

（白圭）说：“不可以，陶器会不够用的。”

（孟子）说：“那个貉国，五谷不能生长，只有黍子能生长；没有城墙、宫室、宗庙和祭祀的礼仪，没有诸侯之间赠礼宴请之类的交际往来，没有各种官吏、官署，所以二十抽一的税率也足够了。而现在你居住在中原，如果抛弃人伦，废掉官吏，那怎么能行呢？

制作陶器的人少了，尚且不能把国家治好，何况没有官吏呢？想使税率比尧、舜的标准还低，是大大小小像貉那样的国家；想使税率比尧、舜的标准还高的，是大大小小像桀那样的暴君。”

【解读】本章是交流税率高低多寡的对话。白圭曾做过魏国国相，是一个能人，而且为人仁爱，自奉甚俭。他想为百姓做好事，打算按照二十税一的比率来征收。他应该没想到孟子会不同意他的意见，因为他知道孟子主张仁政学说，“薄赋税”也在情理之中。孟子从客观现实考量，毫不客气地指出，这种做法在落后小国可以行得通，在中原文明大国则不行。因为二十税一的做法，虽然减轻了百姓负担，但这将影响到国家机器的正常运转，社会秩序保障不了就会产生各种矛盾，最后牺牲的还是百姓的利益；反之，税率多了，国家聚敛财富，虽然保障了国家机器的正常运转，但老百姓的负担就会加重，百姓就会怨声载道。孟子还是赞同要根据各地的实际情况，做到无过无不及，恰到好处。追根究底，这里体现出的还是儒家的中庸之道。

12.11

白圭曰："丹之治水[1]也愈于禹。"

孟子曰："子过矣。禹之治水，水之道也。是故禹以四海为壑[2]，今吾子以邻国为壑。水逆行，谓之泽[3]水。泽水者，洪水也，仁人之所恶也。吾子过矣。"

Bai Gui said, "My management of the waters is superior to that of Yu."

Mencius replied, "You are wrong, sir. Yu's regulation of the waters was according to the laws of water. He therefore made the four seas their receptacle, while you make the neighbouring states their receptacle. Water flowing out of its channels is called an inundation. Inundating waters are a vast waste of water, and what a benevolent man detests. You are wrong, my good sir."

【注释】［1］丹之治水：朱熹《孟子集注》："赵氏曰：'当时诸侯有小水，白圭为之筑堤，壅而注之他国。'"［2］壑（hè）：本义为沟壑，这里指受水处。［3］洚（jiàng）：洪水泛滥。

【译文】白圭说："我治理水比大禹还强。"

孟子说："你错了。大禹治理水患，是顺着水流的规律而疏导。因此禹是以四海作为沟壑，现在您却把邻国作为沟壑。水一旦被堵塞形成倒流，叫作洪水泛滥。使洪水泛滥的人，其行为本身好比洪水，是仁慈的人所厌恶的。您完全错了。"

【解读】本章故事很耐人寻味。白圭自我感觉很有能耐，善于治水，尤其在筑堤治水方面，更是感到很有经验和成就。本章中他和孟子对话，意思是征求孟子的看法。孟子直言不讳地指出他的错误，说大禹治水，是顺水之

以邻为壑　韦辛夷 绘

性，因地制宜，重在“疏导”；而白圭治水，是围堵大水，高筑堤防，重在“堵塞”，危害邻国。一个是利国利民，一个是损人利己，两者虽然同功，但不同效，有着天壤之别，自然无法相提并论，“治水愈于禹”可谓可笑至极。真正实施仁政的人来处理自然灾难，既要有利于自己的国家，也要不危害邻国。“以邻为壑”后来成为成语，流传至今，我们应该以此为戒，切莫只图自己一方的利益，把困难或祸害转嫁给别人。

12.12

孟子曰："君子不亮[1]，恶乎执？"

Mencius said, "If a scholar have not faith, how shall he take a firm hold of things?"

【注释】［1］亮：同"谅"，诚信。

【译文】孟子说："君子不讲求诚信，还会有什么操守呢？"

【解读】本章中孟子说："君子不亮，恶乎执？"孟子在《离娄下》中则曾说："大人者，言不必信，行不必果，惟义所在。"这似乎难以理解，有自相矛盾的嫌疑。那么，"亮（谅）"与"信"之间有着怎样的差别呢？仔细品味两者就会发现，前者孟子把诚信视为人与人之间最基本的道德要求，是安身立命的基石，

是为人处世的底线。后者是讲做人在大是大非面前品质的体现，究其根本归于“惟义所在”，两者是辩证的统一。也就是说，诚信是可以变通的，不要拘泥于小节，面对时局的变化并非一成不变，特别是在“义”字面前。孔子也曾言“人而无信，不知其可也”，却又说“言必信，行必果，硁硁然小人哉”，其中也体现着同样的变通。

12.13

鲁欲使乐正子为政。

孟子曰："吾闻之，喜而不寐。"

公孙丑曰："乐正子强乎？"

曰："否。"

"有知虑乎？"

曰："否。"

"多闻识乎？"

曰："否。"

"然则奚为喜而不寐？"

曰："其为人也好善[1]。"

"好善足乎？"

曰："好善优于天下[2]，而况鲁国乎？夫苟好善，则四海之内，皆将轻[3]千里而来告之以善。夫苟不好善，则人将曰：'訑訑[4]，予既[5]已知之矣。'訑訑之声音颜色，距[6]人于千里之外。士止于千里之外，则谗谄面谀之人至矣。与谗谄面谀之人居，国欲治，可得乎？”

The prince of Lu wanting to commit the administration of his government to the disciple Yuezheng.

Mencius said, “When I heard of it, I was so glad that I could not sleep.”

Gongsun Chou asked, “Is Yuezheng a man of vigour?”

Mencius answered, “No.”

“Is he wise in council?”

Mencius said, “No.”

“Is he possessed of much information?”

Mencius said, “No.”

“What then made you so glad that you could not sleep?”

“He is a man who loves what is good.”

“Is the love of what is good sufficient?”

Mencius said, “The love of what is good is more

than a sufficient qualification for the government of the kingdom; —how much more is it so for the state of Lu! If a minister love what is good, all within the four seas will count 1,000 *li* but a small distance, and will come and lay their good thoughts before him. If he do not love what is good, men will say, 'How self- conceited he looks? He is saying to himself, I know it.' The language and looks of that self-conceit will keep men off at a distance of 1,000 *li*. When good men stop 1,000 *li* off, calumniators, flatterers, and sycophants will make their appearance. When a minister lives among calumniators, flatterers, and sycophants, though he may wish the state to be well governed, is it possible for it to be so?"

【注释】[1]好善：此处指喜欢听取善言。[2]优于天下：足以治理天下。优：充分，足够。[3]轻：容易，不以为难。[4]訑（yí）訑：自满自大的样子。[5]既：全，都。[6]距：同

“拒”，拒绝。

【译文】鲁国想要让乐正子执政。

孟子说：“我听说这件事后，高兴得睡不着觉。”

公孙丑问：“乐正子的能力很强吗？”

（孟子）说：“不是。”

（公孙丑问：）“有智慧有谋略吗？”

（孟子）说：“不是。”

（公孙丑问：）“见多识广吗？”

（孟子）说：“不是。”

（公孙丑问：）“既然这样那么您为什么高兴得睡不着觉呢？”

（孟子）回答说：“他做人喜欢听取善言。”

（公孙丑问：）“喜欢听取善言就够了吗？”

（孟子）说：“喜欢听取善言足以治理天下，更何况治理鲁国呢？如果喜欢听取善言，那么天下的人会不远千里来将善言告诉他；如果不喜欢听取善言，那么人们将会学他说，‘呵呵，我自己早就全知道了！’呵呵的音调和他的脸色已经把人拒绝在千里之外了。士人停止在千里之外，那些喜欢进谗言、阿谀奉承的人就会来到。与那些喜欢进谗言、阿谀奉承的人一起相处，又想把国家治理好，有这可能吗？”

【解读】本章强调为政者要善于听取意见。治国理政，不单要靠为政者的能力、智慧、学识，还应靠集思广益，听取和采纳别人的意见。为什么呢？能够听取别人意见，真正的有识之士就会投奔而来，于是就会人才辈出，在他们有效的辅助下国家就会兴旺；不能听取别人的真知灼见，有识之士就会被拒之于门外，奸佞之徒就会乘虚而入，国家就会败落。

喜欢听善言的人，胸怀一定要宽广，做到“宰相肚里能撑船”。因为真正的“善言”

并非都是好听的话，正所谓良药苦口利于病，忠言逆耳利于行。从这个意义上来讲，这里的“好善”也就是“喜欢忠言”。唐太宗李世民是历史上有名的明君，他和谏臣魏徵的故事几乎家喻户晓，李世民也是“好善”的优秀代表之一，但是即使他是历史少有的好皇帝，不是也有几次冒出想杀掉“善言”频出的魏徵吗？由此可见，乐正子“好善”是一种优良的治国品质。故而，当孟子听说能让乐正子执政，高兴得睡不着觉就不难理解了。“好善优于天下”，这是亘古不变的治国哲学。

12.14

陈子[1]曰："古之君子何如则仕？"

孟子曰："所就三[2]，所去三。迎之致敬以有礼，言将行其言也，则就之；礼貌未衰[3]，言弗行也，则去之。其次，虽未行其言也，迎之致敬以有礼，则就之；礼貌衰，则去之。其下，朝不食，夕不食，饥饿不能出门户。君闻之曰：'吾大者不能行其道，又不能从其言也，使饥饿于我土地，吾耻之。'周[4]之，亦可受也，免死而已矣。"

The disciple Chen said, "What were the principles on which superior men of old took office?"

Mencius replied, "There were three cases in which they accepted office, and three in which they left it. If received with the utmost respect and all polite observances, and they could say to themselves that the prince would carry their words into practice, then they took office with him. Afterwards, although there might be no remission in the polite demeanour of the prince, if their words were not carried into practice, they would leave him. The second case was that in which, though the prince could not be expected at once to carry their words into practice, yet being received by him with the utmost respect, they took office with him. But afterwards, if there was a remission in his polite demeanour, they would leave him. The last case was that of the superior man who had nothing to eat, either morning or evening, and was so famished that he could not move out of his door. If the prince, on hearing of his state, said, '1 must fail in the great point, —that of carrying his doctrines into practice, neither am I able to follow his words, but I am ashamed to allow him to die of want in my country;' the assistance offered in such a case might be received, but not beyond what was sufficient to avert death."

【注释】［1］陈子：即陈臻，孟子的学生。［2］所就三：朱子《四书章句集注》具体归纳为“见行可之仕”“际可之仕”和“公养之仕”三类。就：就职。［3］礼貌未衰：礼仪态度没有衰减之意。［4］周：接济。

【译文】陈子问道：“古代的君子怎样才肯做官？”

孟子说：“去做官有三种情况，辞官也有三种情况。迎接时恭敬而合礼仪，按他所说的话去执行，那就去做官；礼仪态度没有衰减，却不再按他说的去做了，那就辞去官职。其次，虽然没有按他说的去做，但也恭敬礼貌地以礼相迎，那就去做官；一旦礼仪态度衰减了，那就辞去官职。最差的是，早上不吃饭，晚上也不吃饭，饿得出不了门。君主知道后说：‘我在大政方针上不能实行他的主张，又不能听取他的言论，致使他在我的国土上又饥又饿，对此我感到羞耻。’于是周济他，这也是可以接受的，是为了免于饿死罢了。”

【解读】本章指出读书人“就仕”与“去仕”的三种标准。儒家强调修身、齐家、治国平天下，读书增长才干，修身达到致远，然后出来为官。继而，推行自己的政治理想，实施自己的远大抱负，这是每个读书人的终极理想。但凡事都要有原则，孟子给出了读书人做官和辞官的三条道路，这也成为后代知识分子出入进退的原则与标准。

第一种是铮铮铁骨之人，受到尊敬且又能够实施自己的主张，应该出仕做官；一旦只有礼遇，却不能实现自己的理想，便立即走人，正应对孔子所说，“以道事君，不可则止”。这种人个性十足，桀骜不驯，孟子当属其列，他在齐国位列三卿，因齐王不能采用他的仁政主张而决然离开。

第二种是以人格为主之人，既然受到尊

敬，至于自己的主张一时没有被采纳也可以出仕做官；假如人格受辱，官不做也罢，孔子在鲁、卫的遭遇就是这样。这种人温文尔雅，性情大度。

第三种是以生存为主之人，这种人不到饿得不能出门的地步也不会接受周济，周济只是为了免死，所以也不会无限制地接受周济。接受周济的原因，既有君主本该周济的义务，又有君主能够说出悔过之言。这三种人虽然境界有高有低，但还都是有节操、守原则的可敬之士。

12.15

孟子曰："舜发于畎亩[1]之中，傅说举于版筑[2]之间，胶鬲举于鱼盐之中，管夷吾举于士，孙叔敖举于海，百里奚举于市。故天将降大任于是人也，必先苦其心志，劳其筋骨，饿其体肤，空乏其身，行拂乱其所为，所以动心忍性，曾[3]益其所不能。人恒过，然后能改；困于心，衡[4]于虑，而后作；征[5]于色，发于声，而后喻。入则无法家拂士[6]，出则无敌国外患者，国恒亡。然后知生于忧患而死于安乐也。"

Mencius said, "Shun rose from among the channelled fields. Fu Yue was called to office from the midst of his building frames; Jiaoge from his fish and salt; Guan Yiwu from the hands of his gaoler; Sunshu Ao from his hiding by the seashore; and Baili Xi from the marketplace. Thus, when

Heaven is about to confer a great office on any man, it first exercises his mind with suffering, and his sinews and bones with toil. It extreme poverty. It confounds his undertakings. By all these methods it stimalates his mind, hardens his nature, and supplies his incompetencies. Men for the most part err, and are afterwards able to reform. They are distressed in mind and perplexed in their thoughts, and then they arise to vigorous reformation. When things have been evidenced in men's looks, and set forth in their words, then they understand them. If a prince have not about his court families attached to the laws and worthy counsellors, and if abroad there are not hostile states or other external calamities, his kingdom will generally come to ruin. From these things we see how life springs from sorrow and calamity, and death from ease and pleasure."

【注释】［1］畎（quǎn）亩：田间，农田。［2］

版筑：一种筑墙工作，在两块墙版中，填泥土夯实。[3]曾：同“增”，增加。[4]衡：通“横”，指横塞。[5]征：显现，表现。[6]法家拂（bì）士：法家有法度的大臣。拂士：即辅佐的贤士。拂：同“弼”，辅佐。

【译文】孟子说：“舜被举荐于田间劳动之中，傅说被推举于筑墙的人之中，胶鬲被选拔于贩卖鱼盐的人之中，管仲被提拔于囚犯之中，孙叔敖在偏远的海边被选拔任用，百里奚从市场上被选拔出来。所以上天将要把重大责任交给某个人，必定先使他的内心意志受到磨炼，使他的筋骨受到劳累，使他的身体受到饥饿，使他整个身心饱受穷困之苦，做事总是不能顺利，用这样的方式触动他的心志，坚韧他的性情，增长他之前所不具备的才能。人常常犯错误，然后才能改正；心志感到困顿，思虑受到阻塞，然后才能奋起振作；表现在脸色上，生发在声音中，然后才能让人明白

生于忧患，死于安乐　梁文博 绘

了解。一个国家在内缺乏守法度的大臣和辅佐的贤士，在外没有敌对国家的威胁和忧患，这个国家一定会灭亡。这就可以知道，国家在忧患之中往往能够生存下去，处于安乐之中则会走向灭亡。”

【解读】本章是千古名篇，论述了“生于忧患而死于安乐”的道理。孟子连举六个古代杰出的人物，对他们卓越的品性和非凡的精神力量表达了由衷地钦佩和赞赏。六个杰出人士，不是生而知之，不是生而成名，但伟大人物肩负着历史使命，自觉地承担起“天降大任”。他们经历了下层社会生活的艰辛，其卑微的社会地位又使他们遭受鄙视甚至各种屈辱，正是这些长期的困苦经历磨砺了他们的意志，使之坚韧情性、增长才干。正是他们高远的志向追求，让他们在现实挫折中战胜心意困苦，克服思路阻塞，然后吸取教训，改正错误，冲破束缚，奋发有为，最终成长为真正杰出的人才，成就了伟大的事业。

人是这样，国家也是这样，如果国家没有铁面无私、严守法度的大臣，没有人敢于对国家政治进行监督和批评，又没有敌国外患压力，这个国家往往容易垮掉，走向灭亡。逆境和忧患刺激人们奋发图强，努力发展和壮大自己，而长期处于安乐环境之中，人们容易懈怠，追求享乐，人心容易涣散，从而使国家走向衰落。刘邦率兵攻克咸阳，假如刘邦安于王宫享乐，不思进取，很可能会功亏一篑，大汉难立。“生于忧患而死于安乐”，孟子的见解无论是在古代还是在现代，都在一直激励着无数志士仁人在逆境中奋起、在忧患中作为。

12.16

孟子曰："教亦多术[1]矣，予不屑之教诲也者，是亦教诲之而已矣。"

Mencius said, "There are many arts in teaching. I refuse, as inconsistent with my character, to teach a man, but I am only thereby still teaching him."

【注释】［1］术：方式，方法。

【译文】孟子说："教育也是有多种方式的，我对于某个人不屑去教诲，这本身也是一种教诲。"

【解读】本章论及一种特殊的教育方式：不教而教。孟子与孔子一样，都是大教育家，弟子众多，贤人辈出。孔子主张"因材施教"，什么是仁，什么是孝，孔子没有提供统一的标准答案，而是根据提问者的实际情况来回答。孟子强调“得天下英才而教育之”，但天下英才毕竟是少数，可遇不可求。很多人是凡人，甚至是庸才。至于那种不求上进自甘堕落的人，孟子不屑于教，采取的教育方式是不教，让这种吃闭门羹的人受到羞辱与刺激，进而使之幡然醒悟，这不也是很好的教育方式吗?

后记

“中华优秀传统文化书系”是山东省委宣传部组织实施的 2019 年山东省优秀传统文化传承发展工程重点项目，由山东出版集团、山东画报出版社策划出版。

“中华优秀传统文化书系”由曲阜彭门创作室彭庆涛教授担任主编，高尚举、孙永选、刘岩、郭云鹏、李岩担任副主编。特邀孟祥才、杨朝明、臧知非、孟继新等教授担任学术顾问。书系采用朱熹《四书章句集注》与《十三经注疏》为底本，英文对照主要参考理雅各（James Legge）经典翻译版本。

《孟子》（三）由郭云鹏担任执行主编；

刘建、周茹茹、张博、李金鹏担任主撰；王明朋、王新莹、朱宁燕、朱振秋、束天昊、张勇、陈阳光、尚树志、房政伟、屈士峰、高天健、郭耀、黄秀韬、曹帅、龚昌华、韩振、鲁慧参与编写工作；于志学、吴泽浩、张仲亭、韩新维、岳海波、梁文博、韦辛夷、徐永生、卢冰、吴磊、杨文森、杨晓刚、张博、李岩等艺术家创作插图；本书编写过程中参阅了大量资料，得到了众多专家学者的帮助，在此一并致谢。